MW01026119

The
PILGRIM ROAD
insights from the early christians

compiled by david w. bercot

SCROLL
PUBLISHING

The Pilgrim Road. Copyright © 1991 by David W. Bercot. All rights reserved. Published by Scroll Publishing Company, P. O. Box 6175, Tyler, TX 75711.

ISBN: 092-4722-045

Library of Congress Catalog No. 91-060673

Printed in the United States of America

To Leonard Ravenhill,
a pilgrim

Contents

Part Two

Introduction

During the second and third centuries (A.D. 100-300), Christianity was an illegal, persecuted religion throughout most of the civilized world. In many ways, this was a blessing. To a large degree, persecution culled out superficial Christians and those who were not willing to make sacrifices for Christ. It also produced a considerable number of fervent Christians who loved God with their whole heart, soul, and mind — Christians who scorned both the fierce persecutions brought by Satan and the alluring pleasures of this world.

Yet, the persecution of those past centuries has blessed today's Christians as well. That's because the spiritual pilgrims of that era have left us a rich legacy of vibrant writings that provide keen insight on how to walk down the narrow pilgrim way. *The Pilgrim Road* is a unique handbook, collecting together the best insights, reflections, and practical counsel of the early Christians on godly living and complete devotion to God.

This book has been purposefully designed as a devotional work, with a minimum of passages that contain doctrinal discussions. In fact, the editor has generally omitted from this book any phrases, sentences, and paragraphs that are doctrinal in nature. This is because the purpose of this book is to convey the early Christian insights on Christian living — not their theological beliefs. The primary two exceptions to this rule are the early Christian views on salvation and man's free will, which are often inextricably woven into their counsel on godly living.

Because this book is designed to be read as a devotional work, not as a reference book or theological compilation, all quotations are simply credited to the names of their authors, without any reference to the titles of the works from which the quotations have been taken. (All quotations credited simply to "Clement" refer to Clement of Alexandria.) In keeping with the devotional nature of this work, we have not used ellipses to indicate deletions from the original text. Instead, we ask the reader to remember that many of the quotations used in this work are abridgments of the original passages. However, in our abridgments, we have been extremely careful to in no way misrepresent the original message of the authors. Finally, all Scripture citations have been supplied by the editor.

You should find the resulting work both readable and inspirational. Of course, some portions of this work will speak more powerfully into your life than others. So we encourage you to dwell on those chapters that minister to you the most. And since there is no logical progression of chapters, this book can be read in any order.

Please remember that the inclusion of quotations from a particular early Christian writer does not mean that we endorse everything written by that person. Origen is a prime example. In some of his works, he occasionally went off on theological speculations that were not representative of orthodox early Christian thought. On the other hand, probably no other early Christian writer has suffered from such a steady campaign of misinformation as has Origen. Persons who have never read even one line of his works have sometimes already formed negative opinions about the man.

Hopefully, the passages from Origen in *The Pilgrim Road* will allow the reader to become acquainted with the spiritual side of Origen. Few, if any, of Origen's critics have lived his godly, consecrated life, nor would they be willing to undergo the unspeakable tortures that he endured out of his deep love for Christ. We do not condone Origen's theological errors; yet, neither do we hastily judge such a fellow pilgrim.

The excerpts used in *The Pilgrim Road* have been collected, edited, and rendered into readable, contemporary English by David W. Bercot from the translations made for *The Ante-Nicene Christian Library*. Mr. Bercot obtained his Bachelor of Arts degree summa cum laude from Stephen F. Austin University and his Doctor of Jurisprudence degree cum laude from Baylor University School of Law. The early Christian writings have been his special field of study for a number of years. He is the author of the book, *Will The Real Heretics Please Stand Up,* a challenging introduction to early Christianity. He has also written articles for various journals about the early church, and he frequently lectures on the subject of early Christianity.

May these passages bless you as you tread the narrow pilgrim road!

1

The Quotable Pilgrim

To yield and give in to our sinful desires is the lowest form of slavery. To rule over such desires is the only true freedom. **Justin Martyr**

It is better for a man to be silent and yet be a Christian, than to talk and not be one. **Ignatius**

It is good to teach, if he who teaches also acts. **Ignatius**

If we remain ignorant of God, we do not injure him. Rather, we deprive ourselves of his friendship. **Justin Martyr**

If you bear God's *name* but do not possess his *power*, it will be in vain that you bear his name. **Hermas**

If we are not ready to die into Christ's sufferings, his life is not in us. **Ignatius**

Rather than laying down our souls for money, we lay down our money for our souls. **Tertullian**

It is better for me to die on behalf of Jesus Christ, than to reign over all the ends of the earth. **Ignatius**

When the body is deprived of food, drink, and clothing, it dies. But it suffers no harm at all in being deprived of sinful desires. **Justin Martyr**

Sound doctrine does not enter into the heart that is hardened and disobedient. **Justin Martyr**

Prosperity consists of nothing else than to live according to truth. **Justin Martyr**

Always speaking well of the deserving, but never ill of the undeserving, we shall attain to the glory and kingdom of God. **Irenaeus**

The business of the Christian is nothing else than to be ever preparing for death. **Irenaeus**

If someone has the means of doing good to his neighbors, yet does not do so, he shall be considered a stranger to the love of the Lord. **Irenaeus**

How much better it is for men from the very start to not desire forbidden things than to obtain their desires. **Clement**

God made the other works of creation merely by his word of command. Man, however, he framed by Himself, by his own hand. And he breathed into man that which was peculiar to Himself. **Clement**

If the bit of glass is so precious, what must the true pearl be worth? Are we not called on, then, to most joyfully lay out as much for the true crown as others do for the false? **Tertullian**

He who gives to no one becomes poorer. **Clement**

Who can be poor if he is rich toward God? Rather, he is poor who, having much, craves still more. **Mark Felix**

That which is supplied by the work of Christ cannot be exhausted. **Cyprian**

Each of us who sins with his own free will chooses punishment. The blame lies with him who chooses. God is without blame. **Clement**

Love is nothing more than desiring to do good to one's neighbor for the neighbor's sake. **Clement**

We who seek the heavenly bread must rule the belly, which is beneath heaven. **Clement**

Instead of embellishing the outward man with adornments, we should embellish the soul with the ornament of goodness. **Clement**

Those who glory in their looks, not in their hearts, dress to please others. **Clement**

"Render Caesar's things to Caesar and God's things to God." (Luke 20:25) That is, give to Caesar the image of Caesar, which is on the coins. And give the image of God, which has been imprinted on man, to God. In other words, render money to Caesar, but give *yourself* to God. For if you give everything to Caesar, what is left to give God? **Tertullian**

The Church, which is the true temple of God, does not consist of walls, but of the hearts and faith of men who believe on Him. **Lactantius**

If you take away the adornments from wealthy women, and take away the domestic servants from masters, you will find that such people are in no respects different from bought slaves. **Clement**

The wife who loves her husband must be furnished similarly to her husband to travel through this life. If she carries simplicity and chaste seriousness, she has sufficient provisions for the journey to heaven. **Clement**

We are philosophers, not in words, but in deeds. We do not wear our wisdom in our garb, but in our deeds. **Cyprian**

We have no country on earth, and this enables us to scorn earthly possessions. **Clement**

The leg does not feel the chain when the mind is in heaven. **Tertullian**

The proper dress of the temperate man is what is plain, becoming, and clean. **Clement**

A man in good health should not use his servants to carry him, as though they were horses. **Clement**

Servants are to be treated like ourselves. For they are human beings, just like we are. For God is the same to the free and the bondsman. **Clement**

It is right to supply needs, but it is not good to support laziness. **Clement**

Their preconceived ideas cause them to disbelieve. **Clement**

If a man learns without preconceived ideas, he has ears to hear the truth. **Clement**

The best riches are poverty of desires. **Clement**

Make Christ a partner with you in your earthly possessions, so that he also may make you a fellow-heir with him in his heavenly kingdom. **Cyprian**

The teaching that comes from the Savior is complete in itself, without defect. **Clement**

He who believes the divine Scriptures with certainty, receives in them the voice of God, who gave us the Scriptures. **Clement**

To obey the Logos* [Christ], whom we call the Teacher, means to believe him, going against him in nothing. For how can we take up a position of hostility against God? **Clement**

It is not meager income that ever constitutes poverty. Rather, insatiable *wants* constitute poverty. But the good man, being free from such wants, is truly rich. **Clement**

The very best instruction is useless without a learner with a hearing ear. **Clement**

An enemy must be aided, so that he won't continue to be an enemy. **Clement**

Who is so unrighteous as to disbelieve God, and to demand proofs from God as from men? **Clement**

---

*There is no exact equivalent in English for the Greek word *Logos*. It is usually translated as "Word" (John 1:1), but it also encompasses the ideas of "Reason" and "Mind." The Logos of God is, of course, Christ Jesus.

If someone expects to comprehend all things merely
through his physical senses, he has fallen far from the
truth. **Clement**

Faith must not be inactive and alone. Rather, it should be
accompanied with investigation. **Clement**

Trusting is more than bare faith. For when a person has
believed that the Son of God is our Teacher, he trusts that
his teaching is true. **Clement**

The one who knows God prays in thought during every
hour. For he is allied to God by love. First, he asks for
forgiveness of sins. And secondly, he prays that he may sin
no more. **Clement**

There is a difference between declaring things *about* God,
and declaring God himself. **Clement**

Ignorance starves the soul, but knowledge sustains it.
Clement

The more often we are slain by you, the more in number
we grow. The blood of Christians is seed. **Tertullian**

All people love those who love them. It is peculiar to
Christians alone to love those who hate them.
Tertullian

The greater our trials, the greater our rewards.
Tertullian

The more inclined someone is to maliciousness, the more
ready he is to believe evil. **Tertullian**

Condemn the truth if you have the heart — but only after you have examined it. **Tertullian**

Truth is besieged by the vast army of the enemy. Yet, see how secure she is in her own inherent strength! And naturally so. For she wins over whomever she wants from her very adversaries. **Tertullian**

A man *becomes* a Christian; he is not born one. **Tertullian**

Do we prove the faith by the persons — or the persons by the faith? **Tertullian**

No one is a Christian but he who perseveres even to the end. **Tertullian**

Whenever heretics hit upon any novelty, they immediately call their presumption a "revelation." And they call their own distorted ingenuity a "spiritual gift." **Tertullian**

It is, of course, foolish to judge God by our own human conceptions. **Tertullian**

[Addressing the question of what we will do in heaven:] In the presence of God, there will be no idleness. **Tertullian**

Should the offspring of the Most High mingle with the sons of the devil? **Commodianus**

You abuse the commands of the Lord, yet you call yourself his sons! **Commodianus**

God does not govern souls with reference to the fifty or so years of the present life, but with reference to time unlimited. **Origen**

How can a man say that he believes in Christ if he does not do what Christ commanded him to do? **Cyprian**

He who parts and divides the Church of Christ cannot possess the garment of Christ. **Cyprian**

He that is freed owes obedience to his deliverer. Therefore, we who desire to be Christians should imitate what Christ said and did. **Cyprian**

Mankind should love those things that are dear to God. **Cyprian**

There is no more pleasant food for the soul than the knowledge of truth. **Lactantius**

There is more weight in a small number of wise men than in a greater number of ignorant persons. **Lactantius**

It is irreverent to search into those things that God wished to keep secret. **Lactantius**

Wisdom is virtue united with knowledge. **Lactantius**

Apart from divine providence and power, nature is absolutely nothing. **Lactantius**

Both wisdom and religion flow from the fountain of God. And if these two streams turn aside from him, they soon dry up. For those who are ignorant of him can be neither wise nor religious. **Lactantius**

The things that you teach cannot have any weight unless you shall be the first to practice them. **Lactantius**

It is the course of wisdom to acquire those things that neither humans, nor death itself, can take away. **Lactantius**

Let nothing be pleasurable to your hearing except those things which nourish the soul and make you a better person. **Lactantius**

He who chooses transient things will be without eternal things. He who prefers earthly things will not have heavenly things. **Lactantius**

If anyone thinks that clothes, jewels, and other things that men esteem as being precious are valued by God, he is altogether ignorant of what God is. **Lactantius**

The rewards of evil are temporary; the rewards of godliness are eternal. **Lactantius**

Let no one trust in riches, nor in badges of authority, nor even in royal power. For none of these things make a man immortal. **Lactantius**

A person who does not do what God has commanded shows that he really does not believe God. **Clement**

God makes himself known to those who, after doing all that their powers will allow, confess that they need help from him. **Origen**

There are quite a few persons who hold back from becoming Christians — not because they are afraid of losing their *lives* — but because they are afraid of losing their *pleasures*. **Tertullian**

We are as close to the ears of God as we are to the commandments of God. **Tertullian**

Something can sound very logical and still be false. **Mark Felix**

People tend to accept something as true simply because it is boldly asserted. **Mark Felix**

To be in subjection to the desires of the flesh, and to yield to them, is the most extreme form of slavery. To keep those desires in subjection is the only true liberty. **Clement**

The abundance of words can sometimes appear to be solid proof, but it really isn't. **Mark Felix**

Let it be understood that those who are not living by Christ's teachings are not Christians at all — even though they might profess his teachings with their lips.
Justin Martyr

The primary lesson for life must be implanted in the soul from the beginning. That lesson is to know the eternal God, the One who gives what is eternal. **Clement**

The kingdom of sin cannot coexist with the kingdom of God. **Origen**[1]

---

[1]Origen, *Origen*, trans. and ed. Rowan A. Greer (New York: Paulist Press, 1979), p. 133. Copyright © 1979 by The Missionary Society of St. Paul the Apostle in the State of New York. Used by permission.

2

Prayer Life

*"In every thing by prayer and supplication with thanksgiving
let your requests be made known unto God." Phil. 4:6*

How To Prepare For Prayer

It seems to me that the person who is about to come to
prayer should withdraw for a little and prepare himself,
and so become more attentive and active for the whole of
his prayer. He should cast away all temptation and
troubling thoughts and remind himself so far as he is able
of the Majesty whom he approaches, and that it is impious
to approach Him carelessly, sluggishly, and disdainfully;
and he should put away all extraneous things. This is how
he should come to prayer, stretching out his soul, as it
were, instead of his hands. He should strain his mind —
not his eyes — toward God. Instead of standing, he should
raise his reasoning power from the ground and stand it
before the Lord of all. All malice toward any one of those
who seem to have wronged him he should put away as far
as any one would wish God to put away His malice toward
him, if he had wronged and sinned against many of his

neighbors or had done anything whatever he was con-
scious of being against right reason. And although there
are a great many different positions for the body, he should
not doubt that the position with the hands outstretched
and the eyes lifted up is to be preferred before all others....
And kneeling is necessary when someone is going to speak
against his own sins before God, since he is making supplication for their healing and their forgiveness. **Origen**[1]

The Lord's Prayer

Cyprian, was the overseer or bishop of the church in
Carthage, North Africa from about A.D. 240-250. He eventually
gave his life as a martyr for Christ. Here are some of his insights
on the Lord's prayer:

Christ began his prayer with: "Our Father, who is in
heaven." The new man, born again and restored to God by
God's grace, uses the term "Father" because he has now
begun to be a son.

We pray, "Your will be done, in earth as in heaven." In
saying this, we are not asking for God to do what *He* wills
to do. Rather, we are asking that *we* may be able to do what
God wills. For who can stop God from doing what He wills?
Rather, we are hindered by the devil from obeying God's
will in all things, both in thought and in action. Therefore,
we pray and ask that God's will may be done *in us*. And,
in order for it to be done in us, we need God's good will —
his help and protection. For no one is strong in his own
strength. Rather, he is safe by the grace and mercy of God.

"Give us this day our daily bread." We who have
renounced the world, and have cast away its riches and

pomp in the faith of spiritual grace, should ask only for food and sustenance. He who has begun to be Christ's disciple, renouncing all things according to the word of his Master, should ask only for his *daily* food. He should not ask for a longer period of time. For the Lord says, "Take no thought for tomorrow, for tomorrow shall take thought for itself." (Matt. 6:34) For daily bread cannot be lacking to the righteous man.

"Lead us not into temptation." These words show that the Adversary can do nothing against us unless God has permitted it. Therefore, all of our fear, devotion, and obedience can be turned towards God. After all, nothing is permitted to tempt us unless He also gives us power. When we ask that we may not come into temptation, we are reminded of our infirmity and weakness. Therefore, we ask this, lest anyone should proudly vaunt himself or arrogantly assume anything in himself. And when we say, "Deliver us from evil," there remains nothing further we need to ask. When we have once asked for God's protection against evil, and have obtained it, then we stand secure and safe against everything that the devil and the world can work against us. After all, what fear is there in this life to the man whose guardian is God?

The Teacher of peace and the Master of unity did not want prayer to be made singly and individually. He did not want people to pray for themselves alone. For we do not say, "*My* Father, who is in heaven;" nor do we say, "Give *me* this day my daily bread." A Christian does not ask that only *his* debts be forgiven; nor does he request that only he personally will not be led into temptation and that only he will be delivered from evil. Rather, our prayer is on behalf of all. When we pray, we do not pray just for one person, but for the whole Church. For we, the whole Church, are one.

How wonderful it is, beloved brothers, that the prayer which God taught is so brief — that, in his teaching, he condensed all of our prayer into one saving sentence. For when the Logos of God, our Lord Jesus Christ, came, he came unto all. He gathered alike the learned and unlearned. He preached the principles of salvation to every sex and every age group. He made a concise summary of His teachings so that his hearers would not be burdened with heavenly learning, but might quickly learn what was necessary for a simple faith.

Why Many Prayers Are Never Answered

"You ask and do not receive,
because you ask with wrong motives."
Jas. 4:3

Those who pray should not come to God with fruitless or naked prayers. Prayer is ineffective when it is a barren entreaty beseeching God. Every tree that does not bring forth fruit is cut down and cast into the fire. Likewise, words that do not bear fruit cannot deserve anything from God. For example, when Cornelius the centurion prayed, he had standing to be heard. For he was in the habit of giving alms to the people and of constantly praying to God. So when he prayed about the ninth hour, an angel appeared to him, bearing testimony to his labors, saying, "Cornelius, your prayers and your alms have gone up in remembrance before God." (Acts 10:2,4)

We are as close to the *ears* of God as we are to the *commandments* of God. Observing his commandments is what paves a way to heaven for our prayers. The most important commandment [concerning prayer] is that we do not go up to God's altar before we have resolved any conflict with, or offense against, our brothers. (Matt. 5:22,23) After all, how much sense does it make to approach the peace of God without [our own] peace? How can you ask for the forgiveness of debts when you refuse to forgive others? How can we appease the Father if we are angry with our brother? For, from the very beginning, all anger was forbidden to us. (Matt. 5:21,22) **Tertullian**

"Pray Without Ceasing"

When a person knows God, his whole life is prayer and conversation with God. If he is pure from sins, he will certainly obtain what he wishes. God says to the righteous man, "Ask, and I will give to you. Think, and I will do." If what he asks is beneficial, he will receive it at once. If it is harmful, he will never ask for it. So he will not receive it. In this way, it shall be as he wishes.

To speak more boldly, prayer is conversation with God. Even though we speak in silence, not opening our lips, inwardly we are crying out. And God continually hears all this inward conversation. So also we raise our heads and lift our hands to heaven and set our feet in motion at the closing prayers. As we pray, we try, so to speak, to separate our bodies from the earth. We raise the soul to heaven, winged with yearnings for better things. And so we drive the soul to the region of holiness, casting off the chains of the flesh. For we know quite well that the one who knows God leaves behind the whole world, just as the Jews left Egypt behind. Above all, he wants to be as near as possible to God. **Clement**

When a person believes he will receive from God, his
faith is in itself a type of prayer. It is prayer stored away.
Since any occasion to converse with God is prayer, we
should miss no opportunity to talk to God. **Clement**

Of course, you will never bid farewell to a brother who
has entered your house without a prayer. For the
Scripture says, 'Have you seen a brother? You have seen
your Lord.' (Matt. 25:45) This is especially true if the
visitor is a stranger. For he might perhaps be an angel.
(Heb. 13:2) Furthermore, when *you* are a guest of one of
the brothers, you will surely not partake of earthly
refreshments prior to heavenly ones. Otherwise, your
faith will immediately be judged. How else will you obey
the teaching to say, "Peace to this house" unless you
exchange mutual peace with those who are in the house?
(Luke 10:5) **Tertullian**

How Jesus Set An Example For Prayer

*"And He withdrew from them about a stone's throw,
and He knelt down and began to pray."*
Luke 22:41 NAS

If He who was without sin prayed, how much more
should sinners pray! And if He prayed continually,
keeping watch through the whole night in uninterrupted
prayer, how much more should we keep watch every night
in constant prayer.
Christ entreated the Father on behalf of all, saying,
"Neither do I pray for these alone, but for those also who
shall believe on me through their word. That they all may

be one, as you, Father, are in me, and I in you, that they also may be one in us." (John 17:20,21) See how the Lord's loving-kindness, no less than his mercy, is great in respect of our salvation. For he was not content to only *redeem* us with his blood. But, in addition, he also *prayed* for us! See now what the desire of his prayer was — that we should all abide in absolute unity, as the Father and Son are one. From this, it should be clear what a great sin a person commits when he divides the unity and peace of the body. For Christ knew that dissension cannot come into the kingdom of God. **Cyprian**

The Power Of Prayer

*"The effective prayer of a righteous man
can accomplish much." Jas. 5:16 NAS*

Prayer is the only thing that "conquers" God. But Christ has willed that prayer never be used for evil. All the power He has conferred on prayer is for the cause of good. So prayer only knows how to recall the souls of the departed from the very path of death, to transform the weak, to restore the sick, to free the demon-possessed, to open prison doors, and to untie the bonds that bind the innocent. Furthermore, it washes away faults and repels temptations. It extinguishes persecutions. It consoles the low in spirit, and cheers those in good spirits. It escorts travelers, calms waves, and makes robbers stand aghast. It feeds the poor and governs the rich. It raises those who have fallen, stops others from falling, and strengthens those who are standing.

Prayer is the fortress of faith. It is the shield and weapon against the Foe who watches us on all sides. And

so we never walk unarmed. By day, we are mindful of our
stations. At night, we remember our vigil. We guard the
flag of our General by the weapon of prayer. In prayer, we
await the angel's trumpet. **Tertullian**

When Christians pray, they do not even use the precise
names that divine Scripture applies to God. Rather, the
Greeks use Greek names. The Romans use Latin names.
And everyone prays and sings praises to God as best he
can in his mother tongue. For the Lord of all the languages
of the earth hears those who pray to him in each different
language. He hears only one voice, expressing itself in
different dialects. **Origen**

---

[1]Origen, *Origen*, trans. and ed. Rowan A. Greer (New York: Paulist Press,
1979), pp. 164, 165. Copyright © 1979 by The Missionary Society of St. Paul the
Apostle in the State of New York. Used by permission.

3

The Pilgrim Way

"I beseech you as strangers and pilgrims,
abstain from fleshly lusts, which
war against the soul."
1 Pet. 2:11

The one who knows God is like a person who has been sent on a distant pilgrimage. He uses inns and houses along the way, being careful in using the things of the world and the places where he stops. He leaves behind his own home and property without excessive emotion. He readily follows Him who leads him away from this life. He never turns back for any reason. Giving thanks for his journey, and blessing God for his departure, he embraces the mansion that is in heaven. For the soul who has chosen the best life — the life that is from God and righteousness — exchanges earth for heaven. **Clement**

He who chooses to live well for eternity, will live in discomfort for the present. He will be subjected to all types of troubles and burdens as long as he is on earth, so that in the end he will have divine and heavenly comfort. On the other hand, he who chooses to live well for the present will fare badly in eternity. **Lactantius**

19

If, because of the necessities of life, the one who knows God must spend a small portion of time in providing sustenance, he feels cheated. For some of his attention is diverted by business. Not even in his dreams does he look on anything unsuitable to a chosen man. He is a complete stranger and pilgrim on this earth. He lives in the city, but despises the things in the city which others admire. He lives in the city as though he were living in a desert. (Heb. 11:13-16)

Through the perfection of love, he impoverishes himself so he will never overlook a brother in need. This is especially so if he knows that he can bear want easier than his brother. He considers the other's pain his own grief. If he suffers any hardship by giving out of his poverty, he does not complain. Rather, he increases his generosity. For he possesses a sincere faith that is worked out in everyday life. He praises the Gospel both in thought and in deed. He truly wins his praise "not from men, but from God," by doing what the Lord has taught. (Rom. 2:29)

Drawn by his own hope, he does not taste the good things of this world. Instead, he has a noble disdain for all things here. He pities those who are chastised *after* death, who unwillingly make confession as a result of punishment. In contrast, he has a clear conscience as to his departure, and he is always ready for it. With regard to earthly possessions, he is "a stranger and a pilgrim." (Heb. 11:13) He is mindful only of those things that are his own. But he regards all earthly things as *not* his own. He delights in the Lord's commandments, and partakes of the divine will through knowledge. **Clement**

For truly the first thing is to deny one's self and to follow Christ. Those who do this are carried onward to perfection, having fulfilled all their Teacher has willed. They become sons of God by spiritual regeneration and

heirs of the kingdom of heaven. These are those
first that which shall not be forsaken. **Irenaeu**

The words of the Gospel, although perhaps containing
a deeper meaning, may still be taken in their more simple
and obvious sense — teaching us not to be disturbed with
anxieties about our food and clothing, but to live in
plainness and to desire only what is needed, putting our
trust in the providence of God. **Origen**

Philosophers seek the Way. But they do not find the
Way because they seek it on the earth, where it cannot be
found. Rather, this way of life should be sought in the same
manner in which navigators find their way at sea. If a
navigator does not observe some light of heaven, he
wanders on an uncertain course.

So whoever seeks to hold the right course of life should
not look to the earth, but to heaven. In other words, he
should not follow man, but God. He should not serve these
earthly images, but the heavenly God. He should not
measure things by their effect on the body, but their effect
on the soul. Instead of attending to this earthly life, he
attends to eternal life. **Lactantius**

The Inner Life

*"First clean the inside of the cup and of the dish,
so that the outside of it may become clean also."*
Matt. 23:26

The Logos, who cleanses the soul, must first have been
in the soul. It is after his presence and the cleansing that

proceeds from him that all that is dead or weak in the soul is taken away. As a result, pure life comes to everyone who has made himself a fit dwelling for the Logos, who is considered as God. **Origen**

We read that "the flesh is weak," and we thereby soothe our consciences at times. Yet, we also read that "the spirit is strong." (Matt. 26:41) For both expressions occur in the same sentence. Flesh is an earthly material. Spirit is a heavenly one. Why then are we so prone to make excuses for ourselves? Why do we offer our weak part as our defense? Should we not rather look at our strong part? Why shouldn't it be the earthly that yields to the heavenly? Since the spirit is stronger than the flesh, being of a nobler origin, it is our own fault if we follow the weaker of the two. **Tertullian**

Jesus addressed the Pharisees saying, "Woe to you, scribes and Pharisees, hypocrites! For you make the outside of the cup and platter clean, but within they are full of uncleanness." (Matt. 23:25) Although they devoted great care to external things, they overlooked those things pertaining to the salvation of the soul. Knowing their ruin, the Lord Jesus said that they were careful about external things, but they despised those things which are within. For they were strangers to such things. They did not appreciate that He who made the body made the soul also. **Archelaus**

Union With God

*"He has granted to us His precious and magnificent
promises, in order that by them you might become
partakers of the divine nature." 2 Pet. 1:4*

I think that God is loved with the whole soul by those
who through their great longing for fellowship with God
draw their soul away and separate it not only from their
earthly body but also from every corporeal thing. For them
no pulling or dragging takes place even in putting off their
lowly body (cf. Phil. 3:21), when the time allows them to
take off the body of death through what is supposed to be
death. Then they will hear the apostolic prayer and
statement, "Wretched man that I am! Who will deliver me
from this body of death?"... If such a view seems hard to
any one, then he has not thirsted for God, the Mighty One,
the living God; nor has he longed for God "as the hart longs
for fountains of waters." **Origen**[1]

He that is inflamed with ardor and admiration for
righteousness — he is the lover of the One who needs
nothing. As a result, he himself needs but very little. For
such a one has treasured up his happiness in nothing but
himself and God. And in Him there is neither moth,
robber, nor pirate. Rather, there is the eternal Giver of
good. **Clement**

He who is spiritually blind and dumb lacks understanding. He lacks the keen and untarnished vision that
the Savior confers upon the contemplative soul. He is like
the uninitiated at the mysteries. Or the unmusical at
dances. Not yet being pure, he is not worthy of the pure

truth. Since he is still discordant, disordered, and fleshly, he must stand outside of the divine choir. **Clement**

He says, "Do not be anxious for tomorrow." (Matt. 6:34) This means that the man who has devoted himself to Christ should be self-sufficient. He should be a servant to himself. He should lead a life that provides for each day by itself. For it is not in war, but in peace, that we are trained. War needs great preparation, and luxury craves abundance. But peace and love, simple and quiet sisters, require no weapons nor any undue preparation. The Logos is their sustenance.

For whenever anyone has been carried away from external things by the Logos, his attention is drawn from the body to the spirit. He acquires a clear view of what happens according to man's nature. As a result, he will know that he is not to be earnestly occupied about external things, but about what is proper and peculiar to himself. **Clement**

The one who knows God practices righteousness out of love and for the sake of its own excellence. Suppose then that someone required the one who knows God to choose between either everlasting salvation or knowing God. Now, if these things (which are actually inseparable) could be separated, the one who knows God would choose without hesitation knowing God. He deems such knowledge, which comes from faith, to be desirable for its own sake. The man who is complete practices what is good, not for any personal advantage, but because he judges it right to do good.

By that I don't mean that he does good in *some* things, but not in others. Rather, he is consistent in the habit of doing good — not for glory or for the sake of reputation (as do the philosophers) or for reward from either men or God. Rather he practices what is good in order to spend his life after the image and likeness of the Lord. **Clement**

We do not serve God as though he *needed* our service. Or as though he would become unhappy if we ceased to serve him. Rather, we serve him because we ourselves benefit by our service to God. For we are freed from griefs and troubles by serving the Most High God through his Only-begotten Son, the Logos and Wisdom. **Origen**

"Put off the old man with his deeds, and put on the new man, who is renewed in knowledge after the image of him that has created him." (Col. 3:9,10) Those who do this clothe themselves with the image of their Creator. They thereby raise within themselves a statue in accord with what the Most High desires.

Now, among statue makers, there are some who are marvelously perfect in their art. Others, however, make inferior statues. In the same way, there are some who form images of the Most High in a better manner and with a more perfect skill than others. But by far the most excellent of all of these through the whole universe is that image in our Savior, who said, "My Father is in me." (John 14:10) And everyone who imitates Christ according to his ability raises a statue after the image of the Creator. For by contemplating God with a pure heart, they become imitators of him. **Origen**

When he was asked, "Which is the greatest of the commandments?" the Master said, "Love the Lord your

God with all your soul and with all your strength." (Matt. 22:36-38) He said that no commandment is greater than this, and he said so with good reason. For this is a command about our behavior toward the First and the Greatest — God himself. He is our Father. He is the One who has brought all things into being, and everything exists through him. Everything that is saved returns to him. He has loved us beforehand, and we receive our existence through him. Therefore, it is irreverent for us to regard anything else as being older or more excellent than he.

We are required to deliver only this small tribute of gratitude, [our love,] for the great benefits God gives us. In fact, I cannot imagine any other way to repay God, who needs nothing and is perfect. Yet we gain immortality by the very fact of our loving the Father to the fullest extent of our might and power. Because the more we love God, the more we enter within God.

The second commandment He mentioned, which is no less important, is to "Love your neighbor as yourself." (Matt. 22:39). Please note, in contrast, that you are to love God *above* yourself. **Clement**

So what shall we say about the one who knows God? The apostle asks, "Don't you know that you are the temple of God?" (1 Cor. 3:16) So the one who knows God partakes of divinity. (2 Pet. 1:4) He is already holy. He carries God in his body, and God carries him. The Scripture shows that sin is foreign to him, saying, "Do not look on a strange woman with lust." (Matt. 5:28) This plainly demonstrates that sin is foreign and contrary to the nature of the temple of God.

The temple is both great and small. It is as great as the [whole] church. And it is as small as the individual man who preserves the seed of Abraham. The one in whom God dwells does not desire anything else. By putting away all hindrances and distractions, he opens the heavens through knowledge. He passes through the spiritual entities, past all rule and authority, and touches the highest thrones themselves. **Clement**

Man And God Working Together

"Draw nigh to God, and he will draw nigh to you." Jas. 4:8

"I can do all things through Him who strengthens me."
Phil. 4:13 NAS

Perhaps the Father himself draws to himself every one who has led a pure life, and has reached the conception of the blessed and incorruptible nature. Or perhaps our free will, by reaching the knowledge of the good, leaps and bounds over the barriers, as the gymnasts say. Regardless, it is not without eminent grace that the soul is winged, and soars, and is raised above the higher spheres, laying aside all that is heavy, and surrendering itself to its kindred substance. **Clement**

But the Lord answered their despair by saying, "What is impossible with men is possible with God." (Mark 10:27) Once again, his words were full of great wisdom. A man working by himself to gain freedom from his fleshly desires achieves nothing. But if he plainly shows himself to earnestly desire this freedom, God will give him the power to attain it. God conspires with willing souls. But if they abandon their eagerness, the Spirit who is bestowed by

God will be restrained. For to save those who are unwilling is the role of one who exercises compulsion. But to save those who are willing is the role of one who shows grace.

The kingdom of heaven does not belong to sleepers and lazy people, "but the violent take it by force." (Matt. 11:12) This is the only commendable kind of violence: to force God, and take life from God by force. He knows who perseveres firmly (or violently), and he yields and grants to them. For God delights to be conquered in this way. **Clement**

God does not crown those who abstain from wickedness by compulsion, but those who abstain by choice. It is impossible for a person to consistently love others except by his own choice. The one who is *made* "righteous" by the compulsion of another is not truly righteous. It is the freedom of each person that produces true righteousness and reveals true wickedness. **Clement**

It is said, "Blessed are the pure in heart, for they shall see God." (Matt. 5:8) Yet, the strength of our will is not sufficient to procure the perfectly pure heart. So we need for God to create it. Therefore, he who prays as he should offers this petition to God, "Create in me a clean heart, O God." (Ps. 51:10)

We maintain that human nature is in no way able to seek after God, or to obtain a clear knowledge of him without the help of him whom we seek. And he makes himself known to those who, *after doing all that their powers will allow,* confess that they need help from him, who reveals himself to those whom he approves. **Origen**

God is not involuntarily good, in the way that a fire is involuntarily hot. No, it is completely voluntary on God's part to give good things, whether or not he has been asked. No one is saved against his will, for man is not some inanimate object. Rather, we run to salvation voluntarily and of our own free choice. Man received the commandments so that he could choose for himself what things to do and what things to avoid. God does not do good because he has no other choice. Rather, his free choice blesses those who spontaneously turn to him.

The care that God gives us is not like the service that servants give to their masters. Instead, God bestows his care out of compassion for our weakness. So his care is like the care a shepherd gives to his sheep. Or that a king gives to his subjects. And we must be obedient to our appointed leaders who are commissioned by God to direct us. **Clement**

It is to the advantage of each person to understand his own nature, together with the grace of God. For he who does not understand his own weakness or the grace of God will imagine that the benefit conferred upon him by the grace of Heaven is his own doing. And this imagination produces vanity, which will be the cause of his downfall.

Even some of those who shed the blood of the body of Christ have been made alive by Christ's blood. This is the very great patience of Christ! And if it were not such, and if Christ's patience were not so great, then the Church would never have had Paul as an apostle. **Cyprian**

---

[1]Origen, *Origen*, trans. and ed. Rowan A. Greer (New York: Paulist Press, 1979), p. 42. Copyright © 1979 by The Missionary Society of St. Paul the Apostle in the State of New York. Used by permission.

4

On Spiritual Growth

"But speaking the truth in love,
we are to grow up in all aspects
into Him, who is the head,
even Christ."
Eph. 4:15 NAS

When an immature grape has been plucked, the farmer does not despise it as being useless — even though it is still somewhat imperfect. He is not concerned whether or not such a grape possesses perfect sweetness. Rather, he is immediately joyful that this grape has appeared before all the rest. In the same way, God overlooks the defects of the faithful who possess wisdom, though in an incomplete stage, and who have only a small amount of faith. He does not reject them. Rather, he kindly welcomes and accepts them as premature fruits. He honors the mind that is stamped with virtue, even though it is not yet complete. He makes allowances for a mind such as this, viewing it as forerunner of the future vintage. **Irenaeus**

Holiness

"Be ye holy; for I am holy." 1 Pet. 1:16

As I see it, holiness means complete pureness of mind, deeds, thoughts, and words. In its final degree, it means sinlessness even in dreams. **Clement**

We do not object to pagans building temples suited to the images and altars of their gods. But we do refuse to build lifeless temples to the Giver of all life. For our bodies are the temple of God. Therefore, if anyone defiles the temple of God by lust or sin, he will himself be destroyed for acting irreverently towards the true temple. **Origen**

In general, an unworthy view of God maintains no holiness — whether in hymns, lectures, writings, or teachings. Instead, it produces ideas and notions that are base and grovelling. Therefore, to receive the praises of the crowds is really to receive condemnation. For the crowds are ignorant of the truth. **Clement**

Concerning chastity, the holy Logos not only teaches us not to sin in deed, but not even to sin in our thoughts. We should not even *think* of any evil in our hearts, nor should we look on another man's wife with our eyes to lust after her. **Theophilus**

The Church of the Lord, the spiritual and holy choir, is referred to as a body. So those who are merely *called* Christians, but do not live in accordance with the Word, are the fleshly parts.

Now, this spiritual body, the holy Church, "is not for fornication." (1 Cor. 6:13) Likewise, we are not to apostatize from the Gospel by adopting those things that belong to pagan life. And the one who acts like a pagan in the church, whether in actions, words, or thoughts, commits fornication — both as to the Church and as to his own body. If his conduct is contrary to the covenant, he "is joined to the harlot." (1 Cor. 6:15) He thereby becomes another "body" — one that is not holy. He becomes "one flesh" with something else, living a pagan life and having a different hope.

"But he who is joined to the Lord in spirit" becomes a spiritual body by a different kind of union. The one joined to the Lord is fully a son. He is a holy man — one who knows God. **Clement**

The word "holy" sums up all duties toward God and the entire course of life we are to follow. We must not cling too much to our earthly things, even if they are good. For they are of the flesh. On the other hand, we shouldn't hate them either, even if they are bad. Rather, we must be above both good and bad. We trample the bad things underfoot. And we give the things that are good to those who need them. **Clement**

Consistency

"The wisdom from above is ... without hypocrisy."
Jas. 3:17 NAS

Those of us who have dedicated our lives to Christ should live our entire lives in the same serious manner in which we conduct ourselves when in the assembly. We should actually *be* meek, devout, and loving — not just simply *seem* to be.

I cannot comprehend how some Christians change their conduct and manners with the place they happen to be. They make me think of sea polyps, who make themselves part of the rocks to which they adhere, even changing their colors to match those rocks. Similarly, some Christians lay aside the inspiration of the assembly after they leave it. And they become like others with whom they associate. Having paid homage to the sermon about God, they leave behind what they have heard. Once outside, they foolishly entertain themselves with profane amusements. **Clement**

We are commanded to reverence and to honor Jesus, being persuaded that he is the Logos, Savior, and Leader. By venerating him we venerate the Father. We do not honor them only on special days, as some others do, but we do this continually in our whole life, and in every way. So we hold a festival throughout our whole life, persuaded that God is always at our side. We, therefore, cultivate our fields, praising. We sail the sea, singing hymns. And in all of the rest of our conversation, we conduct ourselves according to discipline. **Clement**

The whole life of the one who knows God is a holy festival. His sacrifices are prayers and praises. He reads in the Scriptures before meals. He offers psalms and hymns during meals and before bed, and he prays also again during the night. By these, he unites himself to the divine choir. **Clement**

We openly promise happiness to those people who live according to the Word of God, who look to Him in all things, and who do all things as though in the presence of God. **Origen**

The total Christian is always serving his natural Lord, the Divine Logos, in his thoughts, words, and deeds. All of his days are the Lord's. So he is always keeping the Lord's Day. **Origen**

Find Yourself A Mentor

Therefore, it is necessary for you who are pompous, powerful, and rich to find a man of God to set over yourself as a trainer and mentor. Have godly respect for someone — even if it's only for one man. Answer to someone — even if it's to only one man. Learn to listen to someone else, though there may be only one other man who speaks candidly to you. His words may be harsh, but they will bring healing. For your eyes should not continue unrestrained. It is good for them to sometimes weep and hurt. This will bring you greater health in the long run.

Likewise, nothing is more detrimental to the soul than uninterrupted pleasure.

Learn to fear this godly man [i.e. your mentor] when he is angry. Be pained at his groaning. Respect him as you learn to put a stop to what causes his anger. Anticipate him when he is pleading against your punishment. Let him spend many sleepless nights out of concern for you, interceding with God for you, influencing the Father with the magic of his familiar prayers. For the Father does not hold out against his children when they beg for his pity. And your mentor will pray for you in a pure manner, held in high honor as an angel of God. He'll be grieved not *at* you, but *for* you. This is sincere repentance. "God is not mocked." (Gal. 6:7) Nor does He give heed to vain words. Only He can search the depths of our hearts. He hears those who are in the fire. He listens to those who pray from in the whale's belly. He is near to everyone who believes, but he's far from the ungodly if they do not repent. **Clement**

Fasting

"When ye fast, be not as the hypocrites." Matt. 6:16

The fasting that you think you observe unto the Lord is not a true fast. So I will teach you what a full and acceptable fast to the Lord is. God does not desire empty fasting. Fasting to God in an empty way will do nothing for a righteous life. So instead offer to God a fast of the following kind:

Do no evil in your life. Serve the Lord with a pure heart. Keep his commandments and walk in his teachings. Let no evil desire arise in your heart. And truly trust in God.

If you do these things, you will keep a great fast — one that is acceptable before God. If you guard against these things, your fasting will be complete.

In addition, you should then do the following: First having fulfilled all that is written, on the day of your fast taste nothing but bread and water. Then calculate the price of the meals which you intended to eat that day. Then give that amount of money to a widow, or an orphan, or to some person in need. Thus you will exhibit humility of mind. **Hermas**

5

Separation From The World

"They are not of the world,
even as I am not of the world."
John 17:16

From the very beginning, this was inculcated as a teaching of Jesus among his hearers: that men should shun the life that is eagerly sought after by the crowds, and instead they should be earnest in living the life that resembles that of God. **Origen**

He who zealously imitates the prophetic life, and attains to the spirit that was in the prophets, he will be dishonored in this world and in the eyes of sinners. For to them, the life of the righteous man is a burden. **Origen**

Brothers, let us willingly leave our sojourn in this present world so we can do the will of him who called us. And let us not fear to depart out of this world, deeming the things of this world as not belonging to us, and not fixing

our desires upon them. The Lord declares, "No servant can
serve two masters." (Matt. 6:24) If we desire, then, to serve
both God and Money, it will be unprofitable for us. "For
what will it profit if a man gains the whole world, and loses
his own soul?" (Mark 8:36) This world and the next are two
enemies. We cannot therefore be the friends of both. (Jas.
4:4) **2nd Clement**

Part company with the pagan, O heretic! So long as
you are a Christian, you are a different man from a
heathen. So give him back his own views on things. After
all, he doesn't accept yours. Why lean upon a blind guide,
if you have eyes of your own? Why be clothed by one who
is naked, if you have put on Christ? Why use the shield of
another, when the apostle gives you armor of your own?
Tertullian

Love Not The World

*"Ye adulterers and adulteresses, know ye not that the
friendship of the world is enmity with God?" Jas. 4:4*

The one peaceful and trustworthy tranquility, the one
security that is solid, firm, and never changing, is this: for
a man to withdraw from the distractions of this world,
anchor himself to the firm ground of salvation, and lift his
eyes from earth to heaven. He who is actually greater than
the world can crave nothing, can desire nothing, from this
world. How stable, how unshakable is that safeguard, how
heavenly is the protection in its never-ending blessings —
to be free from the snares of this entangling world, to be

purged from the dregs of earth, and fitted for the light of eternal immortality. **Cyprian**

Seek After The Real Treasure

"Lay up for yourselves treasures in heaven,
where neither moth nor rust doth corrupt,
and where thieves do not break through
nor steal." Matt. 6:20

You, whom the heavenly army has enlisted in the spiritual camp, follow a discipline that is uncorrupted — one that is chastened in the virtues of true religion. Be faithful in both prayer and in reading [Scripture]. First, speak with God. Then let God speak to you. Let him instruct you in his precepts. Let him direct you. Those whom he has made rich, nobody can make poor.

In fact there can be no poverty to him whose breast has once been supplied with heavenly food. Houses adorned with mosaics of costly marble and ceilings enriched with gold — these things will all seem shabby to you now. For now you know that it is you yourselves who are to be perfected, rather than earthly things. It is you who will be adorned instead. Now you realize that the house in which God dwells as in a temple — in which the Holy Spirit makes his abode — this house is more important than all others. Therefore, let us color this house with the colors of innocence. Let us brighten it up with the light of justice. These adornments will never fall into decay with the passing of time, nor will they be defiled by their gold or their colors becoming tarnished.

Those things that are artificially beautified are perishing. For those things do not contain the reality of

ownership. They can give no abiding assurance to those
who possess them. But the house in which God dwells
remains in a beauty that is perpetually vivid. In it, there
are perfect honor and permanent splendor.

God promises that he will hear and protect those who
loosen the knots of unrighteousness from their hearts.
That is, those who give charitably to the members of God's
household according to His commands. For by hearing
what God commands, they themselves also deserve to be
heard by God. The blessed Apostle Paul, when aided by
the brothers in the dire straits of his affliction, said that
good works are sacrifices to God. He said, "I am full, having
received from Epaphroditus the things which were sent
from you — an odor of a sweet smell, a sacrifice acceptable,
well pleasing to God." (Phil. 4:18) For when one has pity
on the poor, he lends to God. And he who gives to the least,
gives to God. These are spiritual sacrifices to God, an odor
of a sweet smell. **Cyprian**

"Get behind me, Satan! You are an offense to me, for
you are not mindful of the things of God, but of the things
of men." (Matt. 16:23) Peter was called a stumbling block
by Jesus, for his words showed that he was not minding
the things of God. Rather, his words showed he was
minding the things of men. That being the case, what is to
be said about all of those persons who profess to have
become disciples of Jesus yet who do not look to things
unseen and eternal, but instead mind the things of men?
Origen

On Being Citizens Of The Heavenly Kingdom

> *"Therefore, since we receive a kingdom which cannot be shaken, let us show gratitude, by which we may offer to God an acceptable service with reverence and awe."*
> *Heb. 12:28 NAS*

We may also see the truth that all the doctrines of the Jews of the present day are mere trifles and fables, since they do not have the light that proceeds from the knowledge of the Scriptures. In contrast, the doctrines of Christians are the truth, for they have power to raise and elevate the soul and the understanding of man. They persuade him to seek a citizenship in heaven — not here below, like the earthly Jews are seeking. **Origen**

Paul says, "For though there be those that are called gods, whether in heaven or in earth, as there are many gods and many lords, but to us there is but one God, the Father, of whom all things are, and one Lord Jesus Christ, by whom all things are, and we by him." (1 Cor. 8:5,6) But the God of gods calls whom he pleases to his inheritance, through Jesus, "from the east and from the west." (Matt. 8:11) And thus the Christ of God shows his superiority to all rulers by entering into their various kingdoms and summoning men out of them to be subject to himself.

When he says, "To *us* there is but one God, the Father," to whom is he referring? He is referring to himself and to those who have risen up to the supreme God of gods and to the supreme Lord of lords. And who is the one who has risen to the supreme God? It is he who gives whole-souled and undivided worship to Him through his Son — the Logos and Wisdom of God, made manifest in Jesus.

And how do we rise above the worship of other gods, who are really demons? We rise above demon worship by doing nothing that is pleasing to demons. Such a person cannot be induced to combine the service to God with the service to any other "god." He does not serve two masters. Yet, there is nothing seditious in our holding to this view and refusing to serve more than one master. To us, Jesus is an all-sufficient Lord. He himself instructs us, so that when we are fully instructed, he may form us into a kingdom worthy of God. In that way, he can present us to God the Father.

Yet, indeed, in a sense we do separate ourselves and stand apart from those who are alienated from the kingdom of God and who are strangers to his covenants. We do this so that we may live as citizens of heaven, "coming to the living God, and to the city of God, the heavenly Jerusalem, and to an innumerable company of angels, to the general assembly and Church of the first-born, who are written in heaven." (Heb. 12:22,23)
Origen

There are, generally speaking, two laws presented to us. The first one is the natural law of God. The other is the written law of governments. When the written law is not opposed to the law of God, citizens should not abandon it under the pretext of following foreign customs. But when the law of God commands something that is opposed to the written law, reason dictates that we bid a long farewell to the written code and to the desires of its legislators. Rather, we give ourselves up to *the* Legislator, God, and we choose a lifestyle that is agreeable to his Word. However, in doing so, it may be necessary to encounter dangers, countless labors, dishonor, and even death.
Origen

Dying To This World

"Likewise reckon ye also yourselves to be dead indeed unto sin, but alive unto God through Jesus Christ our Lord."
Rom. 6:11

Die to the world and repudiate the madness in it. Live to God! By taking hold of him, lay aside your old nature. We were not created to die. Rather, we die because of our own fault. Our free will has destroyed us. We who were once free have become slaves. We have been sold through sin. Nothing evil has been created by God. We ourselves have manifested wickedness. But we, who have manifested wickedness, are able again to reject it. **Tatian**

"He that loses his life," says the Lord, "will find it." (Matt. 10:39) We can lose our life in two ways. First, we can literally give it up by exposing ourselves to danger for the sake of the Lord. For this is what he did for us. Or we can lose our life by freeing it from fellowship with the normal life of this world. If you will cut loose, withdraw, and separate your soul from the delights and pleasures of this life, you will find your soul again, resting in the long-awaited hope. For this is what the cross means. **Clement**

Not Following The World's Entertainment

"And be not conformed to this world: but be ye transformed by the renewing of your mind, that ye may prove what is that good, and acceptable, and perfect will of God." Rom. 12:2

When a person is seated in a place of entertainment that is totally devoid of God, will he be thinking of his Maker? When there is excited strife there for a charioteer, will there be peace in his soul? When he is caught up in the frenzied excitement, will he learn to be modest? **Tertullian**

You are too much of a weakling, Christian, if you would have pleasure in this life as well as in the next. Or, should I say that you are a simpleton if you think that this life's pleasures are genuine pleasures. Even the [worldly] philosophers consider quietness and rest to be the real pleasures. They find their joy and entertainment in these things. They even glory in these things. In contrast, you long for the goal line, the stage, the dust, and the place of combat!

Please answer me this: Cannot we, who die only with pleasure, live without earthly pleasure? For what is our wish other than that of the apostle? That is, to leave the world and to be taken up into the fellowship of our Lord. (Phil. 1:23) You have your joys where you have your longings!

Nevertheless, perhaps your objective is still to spend this period of existence in enjoyments. Well, then, how are you so ungrateful as to not thankfully recognize the abundant and exquisite pleasures that God has bestowed on you? How can you consider these to be insufficient?

For what is more delightful than to have both God the Father and our Lord at peace with us? What is more delightful than the revelation of truth? Or, the confession of our errors? Or, the pardon of the innumerable sins of our past life? What greater pleasure is there than to have no taste for earthly pleasure? Or, to have contempt for all that the world can give? What greater pleasure is there than to have true liberty, a pure conscience, a contented life, and freedom from all fear of death?

What is more noble than to tread the gods of the nations under foot? To cast out evil spirits? To perform cures? To seek divine revelations? To live for God? These are the pleasures — these are the spectacles — that befit Christians. They are holy, everlasting, and free. View these as your circus games. Fix your eyes on the "race course" of the earth, on the gliding seasons. Yearn for the goal line of the final consummation. Defend the assemblies of the churches. Jump up at the sound of God's signal. Be roused by the angel's trumpet. Glory in the palms of martyrdom.

If the literature of the dramas delight you, then appreciate that we have literature of our own in abundance: a wealth of poetic verses, writings, songs, and proverbs. Moreover, these are not merely fictitious, but are true. Instead of being tricks of art, they are plain realities. Are you attracted to fights and wrestling matches? Well, we have no lack of these, and ours are not of insignificant account. Look! Chastity overcomes immorality. Faithfulness slays treachery. Compassion strikes cruelty. Modesty out-wrestles immodesty. These are the contests we have among ourselves. It is in these that we win our crowns. Would you desire blood, too? We even have that — the blood of Christ. **Tertullian**

6

The Way Of Love

*"By this shall all men know that ye are my disciples,
if ye have love one to another." John 13:35*

Because of love, He [Jesus] came down to earth.
Because of love, he clothed himself with man. For love, he
voluntarily subjected himself to the experiences of men.
He did this so that by bringing himself down to the
weakness of those he loved, he could bring us up to the
measure of his own strength. As he was about to be offered
up as a ransom, he left us a new covenant-testament: "I
give you my love." How great is that love? He gave his life
for each of us — one life for all.

So now he demands that we give our lives for one
another. (John 15:12,13) Therefore, since we have made
this mutual agreement with the Savior that we owe our
lives to our brothers, why should we hoard our worldly
goods any longer? After all, they are transitory, worthless,
and foreign to us. Shall we lock up from each other what
will be the property of the fire after a little while? John
makes a divine and weighty statement when he says, "He
who does not love his brother is a murderer." (1 John 3:15)
Such a person is the offspring of Cain, a nursling of the
devil. He does not have God's compassion. He has no hope
of better things. He is sterile. Barren. He is not a branch

46

of the ever-living heavenly vine. He is cut off, waiting for the perpetual fire. **Clement**

Love Thy Neighbor

"Thou shalt love thy neighbor as thyself." Matt. 22:39

In A.D. 312, Constantine defeated his rivals at the battle of the Milvian bridge and became co-emperor of the Roman Empire. He thereafter professed belief in Christ, and in 313, along with his co-ruler, Licinius, issued the Edict of Milan, granting legal recognition to Christianity, and providing freedom of religion to all Romans. A few years later, a well-educated, godly Christian man named Lactantius wrote a series of essays to Constantine, instructing him in what Christians believed. The following is an excerpt from one of his essays.

What else is the preservation of humanity other than to love a man *because he is a man* — because he is the same as we are? If it is contrary to nature to injure a man, it must be in harmony with nature to help a man. And he who does not help another deprives himself of the title of man.

If another person were caught in a fire, or were buried underneath the rubble of a collapsed building, or were drowning in the sea or a river, wouldn't most people consider it their duty to help him? If, therefore, people think it is part of one's duty to help persons when their life is endangered by calamities, why should help be denied when someone suffers from hunger, thirst, or cold?

Yet, the world makes a distinction between these situations. Actually, they hope that those they rescue from some peril will return the favor someday. But there is little hope of return from helping the needy. So the world thinks that it is a waste of resources to help them.

For example, Cicero advised against any charitable giving at all. He said, "Charitable giving, which proceeds from our estates, drains the very source of our giving. For the more persons you give to, the less you will have to give to others." But if Cicero were alive, I would exclaim to him, "Marcus Tullius Cicero, you have erred from true justice! You have taken it away by your words. For you have measured piety and compassion by what is *practical*. In contrast, we must not bestow our goods on those who can suitably repay us. Rather, we must give them to those who are unable to repay. To practice justice, piety, and compassion is to give to those from whom there is no hope of any return."

So when you select persons to give to, do not look at bodily forms. Throw away such sketches and outlines of justice. Instead, be generous to the blind, the feeble, the lame, the destitute, and others who will die unless you help them. They may be useless to men, but they are useful to God. **Lactantius**

Open your compassion to all who are enrolled as the disciples of God. Don't look contemptuously at personal appearance. Don't be carelessly disposed to only a certain age group. If someone appears to be penniless, or ragged, or ugly, or feeble, don't let your soul fret about it and turn away from him. Our bodies are only a form cast around us. They are the occasion of our entrance into this world, and they allow us to enter into this common school of human- ity. But *inside* of us dwells the hidden Father, and his Son, who died for us and rose with us. **Clement**

Love Leaves No Place For Jealousy

"Love ... is not jealous." 1 Cor. 13:4 NAS

Jealousy — what a gnawing worm of the soul it is! What a disease of our thoughts! What a rust spot on the heart! To be jealous is to turn the blessings of others into one's own grief. It is to make other people's glory one's own punishment.

Other sins have their limit. When a crime is committed, it has boundaries — the completion of the crime. The offense of adultery ends when the act is perpetrated. The robber is satisfied once he gains his loot. But jealousy has no limit. It is an evil that endures continually. It is a sin without end.

It is easy to cure physical wounds. But the wounds of jealousy are hidden and secret. They do not give entrance to the remedy of a healing cure. For they have shut themselves up in blind suffering within the lurking places of the conscience. You who are envious, notice how crafty, mischievous, and hateful you are to those whom you hate with envy. Yet, you are the enemy of no one's happiness more than your own. Whomever it is you attack with your jealousy, he can escape you. But you cannot escape yourself. No matter where you are, your enemy is with you; he is always within your own breast.

To hate those who are happy — there is no medicine that will cure this sickness. Rather, you must be cured by the very thing that has wounded you. You must love those whom you previously used to hate. Bless those whom you used to envy with unjust disparagements. If you are able to follow those who are good, imitate them. But if not, at least *rejoice* with them. Congratulate those who are better than you. Make yourself a sharer with them in united love. Your debts will be forgiven when you yourself shall have forgiven others. Your sacrifices shall be received when you at last come to God in peace. (Matt. 5:23,24) **Cyprian**

Forgiving Others

> *"If ye forgive not men their trespasses,*
> *neither will your Father forgive your trespasses."*
> *Matt. 6:15*

How can a person judge the apostate angels if he himself has become an apostate by not forgiving injuries as the gospel teaches? For the apostle says, "Why do you not rather suffer wrong? Why are you not rather cheated? Yes, you do wrong and cheat" by praying against those who sin in ignorance. (1 Cor. 6:7,8) You seek to deprive such persons of the compassion and goodness of God. The apostle refers to the ones who do you injury as "your brothers." By this term, he is referring both to those in the faith and those who may later be in the faith. For someone who is presently hostile to the faith might eventually become a believer. So the logical conclusion is that we should regard *everyone* as a potential brother even if he is not presently in the faith. **Clement**

Treating Servants As Equals

> *"Masters, do the same things to them [slaves], and give up*
> *threatening, knowing that both their Master and yours is in*
> *heaven, and there is no partiality with Him." Eph. 6:9 NAS*

Taking care of your own personal needs, instead of using domestic servants, is an exercise in humility. For example, you should put on your own shoes, wash your own feet, and rub oil on your body yourself. However, if a servant or another has rubbed you with oil, you should do the same thing for him. For this is practicing equality and fairness. And it is good to practice sleeping beside a sick friend. And you should help the infirm, and supply the material needs of those in want. **Clement**

7

Love Your Enemies

"If you love those who love you, what reward have you?"
Matt. 5:46 NAS

Men of old used to require "an eye for an eye, and a tooth for a tooth." (Ex. 21:24) They used to repay evil with evil. But after the Lord and Master of patience supervened, he united the grace of faith with patience. So now it is no longer lawful to attack another even with words. It is unlawful to even say "fool" without the "danger of judgment." Anger has been prohibited. Our spirits are held in restraint. The ill-tempered mind and hand has been held back. The poison of the tongue has been removed. The Law has found more than it has lost, for Christ says, "Love your enemies, and bless those who curse." (Matt. 5:22,44) **Tertullian**

To love one's enemies does not mean to love wickedness, unrighteousness, adultery, or theft. Rather, it means to love the thief, the unrighteous person, and the adulterer. This does not mean to love his sins, which stain the very name of man, but to love *him* because he is a man and the work of God. **Clement**

Malice is always hateful to the Lord. Most of all is this true when our malice is provoked by the malice of our neighbor. In the light of truth, revenge is convicted of great malice. For what difference is there between the provoker and the one who is provoked? The only real difference is that one came before the other in doing evil. Yet, in the eye of the Lord, each stands guilty of hurting another. For the Lord both prohibits and condemns every type of wickedness. In doing evil, there is no account taken of the order in which it was done. The command is absolute that evil is not to be repaid with evil. (Rom. 12:17) **Tertullian**

Resist Not Evil

"But I say to you, do not resist him who is evil;
but whoever slaps you on your right cheek,
turn to him the other also."
Matt. 5:39 NAS

It has been claimed that in the days of Jesus there were other Jews who rebelled against the Jewish state and they became the followers of Jesus. Yet, such accusers are unable to point out any actions on the part of Christians that speak of rebellion.

Take note that the Jews were permitted to take up arms in defense of the members of their families and to slay their enemies. Accordingly, if a revolt had led to the formation of the Christian community, so that it sprung up from that of the Jews, the Christian Lawgiver would not have altogether forbidden the putting of men to death. Yet, he nowhere teaches that it is right for his own disciples to offer violence to anyone, no matter how wicked.

For he did not deem it to be fitting with his laws, which
were derived from a divine source, to allow the killing of
any individual whomsoever.

Furthermore, had the Christians owed their origin to
a rebellion, they would not have adopted laws of such
exceedingly mild character. For their laws do not allow
them, when it is their fate to be slain as sheep, to on any
occasion resist their persecutors. (Matt. 5:39) **Origen**

The philosophers say that a just man is foolish if he
does not take a wounded man's horse away from the
wounded man, in order to preserve his own life. But I deny
that a man who is truly just will ever be in a circumstance
of this kind. Why should a just man carry on war, and mix
himself with the hatred of others? His mind is engaged in
perpetual peace with men. He who does not seek gain, how
can he be delighted with foreign merchandise or with
human blood? The just man is satisfied with his mode of
living.   He considers it unlawful not only to *commit*
slaughter, but to be present with those who slaughter
others. **Lactantius**

But If We Don't Resist Evil, Who Will?

The pagan critic, Celsus, scoffed at the early Christian stance
of non-resistance, asking the following question, to which Origen
wrote a reply:

Celsus: Surely you do not really believe that if the
Romans were to neglect their customary duties to the gods
and to men, and were to worship the Most High — or
whatever you care to call him, that he would come down

and fight for them so that they would need no other protection than his. After all, this same God promised this sort of thing in past times to the Jews. Instead of being masters of the whole world, the Jews are left with not even a patch of ground or a home.

Origen: If what God promised to those who would keep his law has not come to pass, the reason the promise has not been fulfilled cannot be ascribed to the unfaithfulness of God. That is because the fulfillment of his promises was dependent on certain conditions. The condition was that the Jews had to obey and live according to his law. So if the Jews have not even a plot of ground or a habitation left to them, the entire blame is to be laid upon their sins, and especially upon their guilt in the treatment of Jesus.

But if all the Romans were to embrace the Christian faith, they would overcome their enemies when they prayed. Or, more accurately, they would not war at all. For they would be guarded by that divine power that promised to save five entire cities for the sake of only fifty righteous persons. For men of God are assuredly the salt of the earth. They preserve the order of the world. And society is held together as long as the salt is uncorrupted. (Matt. 5:13)

The Pax Romana

Throughout most of the history of Europe and the Middle East, there have been endless successions of wars. However, during the period from the birth of Christ to A.D. 180, the ancient Mediterranean world enjoyed a period of blessed peace. The Roman Empire did not experience even one successful invasion of its frontiers during this period, which is called by historians "the

Pax Romana." The early Christians believed that this extraordinary period of peace was a result of divine intervention.

There is an abundance of peace, which began at the
birth of Christ. For God was preparing the nations for
Christ's teaching. Accordingly, he arranged for the various
nations to be under one prince, the king of the Romans.
Formerly, the existence of many kingdoms led to the lack
of unity among the nations. This lack of unity would have
made it more difficult for the apostles of Jesus to
accomplish the task given to them by their Master: "Go
and teach all nations." (Matt. 28:19)

Jesus was born during the reign of Augustus, who
fused together into one monarchy the many populations
of the earth. As I have said, the existence of many
kingdoms would have been a hindrance to the spread of
the doctrine of Jesus throughout the entire world. This is
true not only for the reason I have mentioned, but also on
account of the need of men everywhere to engage in war,
fighting on behalf of their native country. For such was
the case before the times of Augustus, and in periods still
more remote, when necessity arose. For example, the
Peloponnesians and the Athenians warred against each
other. And other nations warred in like manner.

How, then, was it possible for the Gospel doctrine of
peace, which does not even permit men to take vengeance
upon enemies, to prevail through the world, unless at the
birth of Jesus a milder spirit had been everywhere
introduced into the conduct of things? **Origen**

8

Obedience And Testing

"Not every one that saith unto me, Lord, Lord, shall enter into the kingdom of heaven; but he that doeth the will of my Father which is in heaven." Matt. 7:21

The man who has the Lord *in his heart* can also be lord of all creatures and of every one of God's commandments. However, these commandments are hard and difficult to those who have the Lord only on their lips. For their hearts are hardened, and they are far from the Lord. **Hermas**

A person who is faithful safeguards the things that have been entrusted to him. He doesn't betray the trust. We Christians have been entrusted with the divine utterances and the divine commands. We also have the obligation to *obey* them. The one keeping this trust is the faithful servant who will be praised by the Lord. **Clement**

He who does not believe God cheats himself out of his own hope. And he who does not do what God has commanded does not believe Him. **Clement**

He said, "Why do you call me Lord, Lord, but do not do
the things which I say?" (Luke 6:46) For 'the people that
love with their *lips* but have their hearts far away from
the Lord' are not the people of the Lord. They trust in
another lord and have willingly sold themselves to him.
But those who keep the commandments of the Lord testify
to Him by their very actions. **Clement**

When we hear, "Your faith has saved you," (Mark 5:34)
we do not understand Christ to be saying *absolutely* that
those who have believed in *any* way whatever shall be
saved, unless good actions follow. No one can be a believer
and at the same time be immoral. **Clement**

What does it mean to follow Christ? He follows Christ
who stands in Christ's commandments. Who walks in the
way of his teaching. Who follows his footsteps and his
ways. Who imitates those things that Christ both taught
and did. **Cyprian**

Christ calls his people "sheep," for their Christian
innocence should be like that of sheep. He calls them
"lambs," that their simplicity of mind may imitate the
simple nature of lambs. To put on the name of Christ —
and yet not go in the way of Christ — what else is it but a
mockery of the divine name? A desertion of the way of
salvation? **Cyprian**

Why We Are Tested

"In this you greatly rejoice, even though now for a little while, if necessary, you have been distressed by various trials, that the proof of your faith, being more precious than gold which is perishable, even though tested by fire, may be found to result in praise and glory and honor at the revelation of Jesus Christ." 1 Pet. 1:6,7 NAS

"God is faithful, and he will not permit you to be tempted beyond what you can bear." (1 Cor. 10:13) In other words, each person is tempted in proportion to the amount of his strength or power of resistance. However, we should not thereby suppose that he who is tempted will necessarily prove victorious in the struggle.

It is like those who fight in the arena. Just because someone is paired with an opponent of equal ability, it does not necessarily follow that he will be the victor. However, unless the abilities of the combatants were equal, the prize of the victor would not be justly won.

But it is up to us to use God's power either with energy or with feebleness. For there is no doubt that we have a power of endurance for every temptation — if only we properly employ the strength that is granted to us. But there is a difference between possessing the *power* to conquer and actually *being victorious*. For the apostle himself demonstrated this by his cautious use of language, saying, "God will make a way to escape, so that you *may* be able to bear it," not that you *will* bear it. For many do not overcome temptation but are overcome by it.

So God does not automatically enable us to endure temptation. If he did, there would be no real struggle. Rather, he gives us the power to endure temptation. Now, in accordance with our faculty of freewill, this enabling power may be used by us either in a diligent manner or in

a slothful manner. If we use it in a diligent manner, then
we prove victorious. If we use it slothfully, we are defeated.

For if this power were given to us in such a way that
we would of necessity be victorious — that we could never
be defeated — there would be little motive for a person to
struggle. After all, he could not be overcome. But if the
possibility of conquering is equally conferred on us all, and
if it be in our own control how to use this power — either
diligently or slothfully — then those who are conquered
are justly condemned and those who are victorious are
deservedly praised. **Origen**

Nothing distinguishes the righteous from the unrighteous more than suffering affliction. Under affliction, the
unrighteous man impatiently complains and blasphemes.
In contrast, the righteous man is proved by his patience.
Cyprian

We will act far more profitably and cautiously if we
hazard the presumption that God provided all of these
ensnaring things in the beginning and that he placed them
in the world as a test to prove the discipline of his servants.
For the freedom of use is perhaps the means by which God
conducts an experimental trial to test our self-control.

Don't wise family heads purposely offer and permit
certain things to their servants in order to test whether
their servants will actually use the things thus permitted?
And to see *how* they will use them. That is, will they use
them honestly? Will they use them with moderation? Yet,
how far more praiseworthy is the servant who abstains
entirely. How far more praiseworthy is the servant who
has a wholesome fear even of the *privileges* allowed by his
lord. As the apostle said, "All things are lawful, but not all

are expedient." (1 Cor. 10:23) How much more readily will
we fear what is *unlawful* when we have a reverent awe of
what is *lawful?* **Tertullian**

Resisting Satan

*"We wrestle not against flesh and blood, but against ...
spiritual wickedness in high places." Eph. 6:12*

The struggle for freedom is not only waged by the
soldiers of battles in wars. Rather, it is also waged in
banquets, in beds, and before the tribunals by those who
are anointed by the Logos — who are ashamed to become
the captives of pleasures. In truth, the kingly man — the
Christian — should be a ruler and a leader. For we are
commanded to be lords over not only the wild beasts of the
field, but also over the wild passions within ourselves.
Clement

"Be sober and watch. For your Adversary the devil, like
a roaring lion, goes about seeking anyone to devour."
(1 Pet. 5:8) The Adversary prowls around all of us. Like an
enemy besieging those who are shut up in a city, he
examines the walls. He checks to see if any part of the
walls is less firm and less dependable. He seeks to enter
through such a weak spot so as to penetrate to the inside.
Therefore, he presents seductive forms and easy
pleasures to the eyes, in order to destroy chastity through
our eyes. He tempts the ears with harmonious music, so
he can relax and weaken Christian vigor through hearing
sweet sounds. He promises earthly honors so he can

deprive us of heavenly ones. He makes a showy display of false things, so he can steal away those that are true.

And when he cannot secretly deceive us, he then threatens us plainly and openly, hoping that fear of violent persecution will conquer God's servants. This is the Adversary — always restless and hostile, crafty in peace but fierce in persecution. **Cyprian**

Man's fear of the Lord is an honor to God. However, that most stubborn Foe never gives his evil any rest. In fact, he is the most savage when he realizes that a man has been freed from his clutches. He ravages the most fiercely at the time he is fast becoming extinguished. He grieves and groans over the fact so many works of death in man have been overthrown by God's grant of pardon. He grieves that the former sinner, who is now Christ's servant, is destined to judge both him and his angels. **Tertullian**

The devil cannot hold power over those servants of God who place their hopes in Him with all their hearts. The devil can wrestle against them, but he cannot overthrow them. Therefore, if you resist him, he will be conquered and will flee in disgrace from you. (Jas. 4:7) It is only those who are spiritually empty who should fear the devil and his power against them.

Suppose a man has filled highly suitable jars with good wine, but that he has left a few jars only half full. Now, when that man passes by the jars, he does not look at the full jars, for he knows that they are unspoiled. Rather, he looks at the half-full jars, fearing that the wine in them may have gone sour. For partially-filled jars quickly become sour, and the goodness of the wine is gone.

Similarly, the devil inspects all of the servants of God in order to test them. But those who are full in the faith resist him strongly. As a result, he withdraws from them, having no entrance. So he goes to those who are only partially filled. Finding an entrance into them, he produces in them whatever he wishes. And they become his servants. **Hermas**

The Christian — the true Christian, I mean, who has submitted to God alone and to his Logos — will suffer nothing from demons. For God is mightier than demons. For "the angel of the Lord will encamp around those who fear Him and will deliver them." (Ps. 34:7) **Origen**

We may see how much power against the harshest sufferings and the deepest tortures there is in religion and in the spell of love for God, which is immensely more powerful than any other love spell. Human weakness does not live in the same city with this spell of love for God, since it is driven abroad from the soul and has no power to act when a person can say, "The Lord is my strength and my song." (Ps. 118:14) and "I can do all things in Him who strengthens me, Christ Jesus our Lord." (Phil. 4:13; 1 Tim. 1:12) **Origen**[1]

---

[1]Origen, *Origen*, trans. and ed. Rowan A. Greer (New York: Paulist Press, 1979), p. 59. Copyright © 1979 by The Missionary Society of St. Paul the Apostle in the State of New York. Used by permission.

9

Repentance

"Do you think lightly of the riches of His kindness and forbearance and patience, not knowing that the kindness of God leads you to repentance?"
Rom. 2:4 NAS

When there is no fear, there is no change of conduct. Where there is no change, there is only a vain "repentance." For it lacks the fruit for which God purposed it — the salvation of man. **Tertullian**

The baptismal washing is a sealing of faith, which faith begins with repentance and is entrusted to repentance. We are not washed *in order that* we may quit sinning. Rather, we are washed in baptism *because* we have already quit. In our hearts, we have already been bathed. For the first baptism of a learner is this — perfect fear. Such a learner has understanding of the Lord, and his faith is sound. His conscience has once for all embraced repentance.

So it is fitting that learners *desire* baptism, but do not hastily *receive* it. For he who desires it, honors it. He who hastily receives it, disdains it. **Tertullian**

True And False Repentance

[At baptism], through repentance, a person renounces God's rival, the devil, and subjects himself to the Lord. Such a person commits a serious sin if he again lifts Satan up by returning to the Enemy. For he gives the devil cause to exult. With his prey recovered, the Evil One rejoices anew against the Lord.

Such a person thereby places the devil ahead of the Lord. For he has been able to compare both God and the devil, having served them both. By choosing to be the devil's servant again, he pronounces the devil to be the better master. He has "repented" of his repentance and made satisfaction to the devil. **Tertullian**

A person who is continually and repeatedly repenting for the same sins does not differ from those who have never believed, except that unbelievers are not aware that they are sinning. And I don't know which of the two is worse. So the frequent asking of forgiveness for those things in which we continually transgress is not true repentance. It is merely the *semblance* of repentance. **Clement**

Repentance is the price the Lord exacts from us before awarding pardon. In the marketplace, sellers first examine the coin with which they make their bargains, to see whether it is cut, scraped, or counterfeited. Likewise; I believe that the Lord makes examination of our repentance when he is about to grant us such costly merchandise — eternal life. **Tertullian**

As soon as you know the Lord, you should fear him. As
soon as you have gazed on him, you should reverence him.
After all, what difference does your knowing him make, if
you continue in the same things you did before you knew
him? **Tertullian**

I want to speak of that most gentle father, who calls
his prodigal son home and willingly receives him back
repentant after the son has squandered all. God, then, will
receive you back, his own son, even if you have squandered
what you had received from him — even if you return
naked. He receives you simply because you *have* returned.
But only if you thoroughly repent. Only if you contrast
your own hunger with the plenty of your Father's "hired
servants." Only if you leave behind the herd of swine, that
unclean herd. Only if you again seek your Father, offended
though he is, saying, "I have sinned and am no longer
worthy to be called your son." **Tertullian**

On The Confession Of Sins

"Confess your sins to one another, and pray for one another,
so that you may be healed." Jas. 5:16 NAS

I allow no place for bashfulness in confessing sins, for
giving up bashfulness profits me. Why do you think your
brothers are anything other than men like yourself?
Among brothers and fellow-servants, there is common
hope, fear, joy, grief, and suffering. That is because there
is a common Spirit from a common Lord and Father. The
body cannot feel any gladness at the trouble of any one

member. Rather, it must of necessity join in the grief with one united voice — as well as joining in to work out a remedy.

In the company of two, there is the church. But the church is the body of Christ. When, therefore, you cast yourself at the knees of your brothers, you are entreating Christ. When your brothers shed tears over you, it is Christ who suffers, Christ who asks the Father for mercy. And what a son asks of his father is easily obtained. If we hide something from the knowledge of man, shall we equally conceal it from God? Is it better to be damned in secret than to be absolved in public? **Tertullian**

10

On Death And Suffering

*"Though I walk through the valley of the shadow of death,
I will fear no evil: for thou art with me;
thy rod and thy staff they comfort me."*
Ps. 23:4

Why Death Exists

An eminent artisan once created a noble statue, made of gold. It was beautifully proportioned in all of its members — exquisite to look upon. But there was an evil man who was so jealous over this beautiful statue that he could no longer bear to see its beauty. So in his envy, he mutilated the statue, destroying its elegance.

Upon discovering this, the artificer decided to cast the statue over again. For he had bestowed much pain, labor, and care upon the statue. And he wanted it to be free from defect. So his only choice was to melt the statue down and then remold it to its original beauty.

Now, God's plan seems to be similar. Upon seeing man, his most beautiful work, corrupted by envious treachery, he could not bear to leave man in such a condition. For he loved man, and he did not want man to remain blemished forever and to carry blame for all eternity. So he dissolves man again back to his original materials. In this way, by remolding man, all of man's blemishes can waste away and disappear.

So the melting down of the statue corresponds to the death and dissolution of the body. And the remolding of the statue corresponds to the resurrection after death. Arnobius

The Resurrection

"Jesus said unto her, I am the resurrection, and the life:
he that believeth in me, though he were dead,
yet shall he live." John 11:25

The revolving order of things around us bears witness to the resurrection of the dead. Day dies into night and is buried everywhere in darkness. The glory of the world is obscured in the shadow of death. Its entire substance is tarnished with blackness. All things become sordid, silent, and dull. Everywhere business ceases, and occupations rest. And so there is mourning over the loss of light.

Yet, it again comes back to life, with its own beauty, its own gift, its own sun. Yes, the same sun as ever, whole and entire, over all the world, returns, slaying its own death — night. It opens its own sepulchre of darkness, coming forth as the heir to itself. Yet, then the night also comes back to life. And it, too, is accompanied with a retinue of its own. For the stellar rays, which had been quenched in the morning glow, are rekindled. The distant groups of constellations are again brought back into view. The mirrors of the moon are re-adorned, which her monthly course had worn away.

In the same manner, winters and summers return, as do the springtime and autumn — with their characteristics, their routines, and their fruits. For earth receives its instructions from heaven to clothe the trees which had been stripped bare. To color the flowers afresh. To spread the green grass again. And to reproduce the seed that has "died" — which cannot reproduce *until* it has died. (John 12:24)

What a wonderful method! In order to restore, it takes away. In order to guard, it destroys. It injures that it may make whole. It first diminishes that it may enlarge. In short, all creation is instinct with renewal. All things begin after they have ended. They come to an end for the very purpose of coming into existence again. So nothing perishes except with a view to salvation. **Tertullian**

We do not maintain that the body that has undergone corruption will resume its original nature in the resurrection — any more than a grain of wheat that has decayed returns to its former condition. Rather, we maintain that, just as a stalk arises from a grain of wheat, so a certain power is implanted in the body, which is not destroyed in death, and from which the body is raised up in incorruption. **Origen**

How Christians Should Respond To Suffering And Death

In the middle of the third century, a severe plague swept through North Africa, killing tens of thousands of people — Christian and pagan alike. In some places, the dead outnumbered the living. Some thought that the end of the world was imminent. Many Christians were surprised that they too were afflicted by this deadly plague. In the midst of this, Cyprian encouraged and challenged his fellow Christians with these words:

In very many of you, dearly beloved brothers, there is a steadfast mind and a firm faith. There is a devoted spirit that is not disturbed by the frequency of this present mortality. You are like a strong and stable rock that shatters the turbulent onsets of the world and the raging waves of time. Yet, like a rock you are not shattered and are not overcome by these trials. Instead, you are tested by them. Yet I observe that some are standing less steadily and are not exerting the divine and unconquered vigor of their heart.

Dearest brothers, he who wars for God should view himself as one who, placed in the heavenly battle camp, already hopes for divine things. So we should have no trembling at the storms and whirlwinds of the world. The kingdom of God, beloved brothers, is beginning to be at hand. The reward of life, and the rejoicing of eternal salvation are now coming. With them come the perpetual gladness and regaining of Paradise that has been lost. Along with them comes the passing away of the world. Already heavenly things are taking the place of earthly things.

So what room is there here for anxiety and worry? Who in the midst of these things is trembling and sad — except for him who is without hope and faith? To fear death is for those who are not willing to go to Christ. And who is unwilling to go to Christ? Is it none other than the one who does not believe that he is about to reign with Christ?

It is written that the just live by faith. If you are just, if you live by faith, if you truly believe in Christ — why don't you embrace the assurance that you are called to Christ? You are about to be with Christ. You are secure in

the Lord's promise. So why don't you rejoice that you are
freed from the devil?

To see Christ is to rejoice. In fact, we cannot have true
joy until we shall see Christ. So what blindness of mind it
is — what folly it is — to love the world's afflictions,
punishments, and tears. Why not rather hasten to the joy
which can never be taken away!

The problem, brothers, is that faith is lacking. No one
believes that the things that God promises are true. Yet,
He *is* true! His word to believers is eternal and unchange-
able. If a serious and praiseworthy man should promise
you anything, you would assuredly have faith in his
promise. You would not think that you would be cheated
and deceived by him. That is, if you knew him to be
steadfast in his words and his deeds. But now it is God
himself who is speaking to you. And do you faithlessly
waver in your unbelieving mind? God promises you
immortality and eternity on your departure from this
world. And do you doubt? If so, this is to not know God at
all. This is to offend Christ.

When Christ's disciples were saddened when He said
that He was soon to depart, He spoke to them and said, "If
you loved me, you would surely rejoice because I go to the
Father." (John 14:28) He thereby taught and demonstrated that when the dear ones we love depart from this
world, we should *rejoice* rather than grieve. In light of this
truth, the blessed Apostle Paul said a similar thing in his
letter: "To me, to live is Christ, and to die is gain." (Phil.
1:21)

However, it disturbs some that the power of this
disease attacks our people the same as the pagans. As if
the Christian believes for the purpose of having the enjoyments of the world and a life free from illness! Rather, we
should believe as one who undergoes all adverse things
here, being reserved for future joy.

It disturbs some that death is common to *us* the same as others. Yet, what is there in this world that is not common both to us and to others? So long as our flesh remains in this world, we are subject to the law of our natural birth. And this birth is common both to us and to them. So long as we are here in the world, we are connected with the human race in fleshly equality. We, however, are separated in spirit. Thus, when the earth is barren with an unproductive harvest, famine makes no distinction. Or, when a city is captured through the invasion of an enemy, all persons alike are taken captive. And when the serene clouds withhold the rain, the drought affects everyone the same. When the jagged rocks tear open a ship, the shipwreck is common to all. The diseases of the eyes, the attacks of fevers, and the feebleness of limbs are universal. These things are so as long as our common flesh is borne by us in the world.

In fact, if a Christian knows and holds to the condition and law under which he has believed, he will be aware that he must suffer *more* than others in the world. For he must struggle more against the attacks of the devil. Righteous men have always possessed this endurance. From the command of the Lord, the apostles maintained this rule: Not to complain in adversity, but to bravely and patiently accept whatever things happen in this world. We must not complain in adversity, beloved brothers, but we must bear whatever happens with patience and courage. For it is written, "The sacrifice to God is a broken spirit, a contrite and humbled heart that God does not despise." (Ps. 51:17)

In such manner, Abraham pleased God. In order to please God, he did not shrink back even from losing his son or from sacrificing him. You who cannot endure to lose your son through ordinary death, what would you do if you were asked to *kill* your son?

Let not these hardships be offenses to you. Rather, view them as battles. Do not let them weaken or break the

Christian's faith. Rather, let the Christian demonstrate
his strength through them. Remember, unless the battle
comes first, there can be no victory.

It is an empty show of faith when there is no danger.
Struggles and adversity are what test the truth about our
faith. The tree that is deeply rooted is not swayed by the
onset of winds. The ship built of strong timbers is not
shattered when the waves beat against it. When grain is
brought to the threshing floor, the strong and hearty
grains scorn the wind. But the empty chaff is carried away
by the gust that hits it.

What a grandeur of spirit it is to struggle with all the
powers of an unshaken mind against so many onsets of
devastation and death! What joy to stand tall amid the
desolation of the human race and not to despair with those
who have no hope in God.

Furthermore, this plague and disease that seems so
horrible and deadly is actually a timely, necessary thing.
It searches out the righteousness of each person. It
examines the minds of the human race to see whether
those in health will tend the sick. Whether persons
affectionately love their relatives. Whether masters pity
their languishing servants. Whether physicians will
forsake the patients who entreat them. Whether the fierce
will suppress their violence. Whether the haughty will
bend their necks. Even if this plague conferred nothing
else, it has benefited Christians and God's servants in this
way: we begin gladly to desire martyrdom as we learn not
to fear death. This is merely training for us — not death.

We must remember that we should do God's will, not
our own. This is in accordance with what our Lord has
directed us to pray for daily. How preposterous and absurd
it is to ask that God's will be done, yet when God calls and
summons us from this world, we do not immediately obey
the command of his will. Instead, we struggle and resist.
Like a stubborn servant, we are dragged to the presence

of the Lord with sadness and grief. So we depart from here under the bondage of necessity, not with the obedience of free will. Yet, we then wish to be honored with celestial rewards by Him to whom we unwillingly come!

Why, then, do we pray for the kingdom of heaven to come, if the captivity of earth so delights us? Why with frequently repeated prayers do we entreat and beg that the day of his kingdom may hasten, if our greater desires and stronger wishes are to obey the devil here, rather than to reign with Christ?

Our brothers who are freed from this world by the Lord's summons should not be lamented. For we know that they are not lost, but are merely sent ahead of us. In parting from us, they simply precede us as travelers and navigators often do. They should be admired, not bewailed. Why should we wear black garments, when they have already put on white garments there?

We give the Gentiles justified grounds to mock us, saying, "You say that the dead are alive with God, yet you mourn for them as though they were extinct and lost." So what we say appears to be pretended, feigned, and counterfeit. What advantage is there to set forth virtue by our *words*, but then destroy the truth by our *deeds?*

If we believe in Christ, let us have faith in his words and promises. And since we shall not die eternally, let us come with a glad security to Christ, with whom we are both to conquer and to reign forever. When we die, we are passing over to immortality by death. In fact, eternal life cannot follow, unless we first depart from this life.

So let us show ourselves to be what we believe: That we do not grieve over the departure of those dear to us. That when the day of our summons arrives, we come without delay and without resistance to the Lord when he himself calls us. And since this is how it always should be done by God's servants, how much more should it be done

now — now that the world is collapsing and is oppressed
with the tempests of mischievous ills.

If the walls of your dwelling were shaking with age —
if the roofs above you were trembling — if the house, all
worn out and wearied, were threatening an immediate
collapse, would you not depart from it with all possible
speed? If you were on a voyage and suddenly the waves
were violently aroused by an angry and raging tempest,
pointing to an imminent shipwreck, would you not quickly
seek the harbor? Look! The world is changing and passing
away. Its ruin is not imminent because of its *age*, but
because the end of things approaches.

We should ever reflect on the fact that we have
renounced the world. We are simply living here in the
meantime as guests and strangers. What person placed in
a foreign country would not hurry to return to his own
country? Who that is eager to return to his friends would
not eagerly desire a prosperous gale that he might
embrace those dear to him even sooner.

We regard Paradise as our country. We already
consider the patriarchs as our parents. So why do we not
hasten and run, that we may behold our country, that we
may greet our parents? There a great number of our dear
ones are awaiting us. There is a dense crowd of parents,
brothers, and children longing for us — already assured
of their own safety but still concerned for our salvation. To
these, beloved brothers, let us hasten with an eager desire.
Let us crave quickly to be with them, and quickly to come
to Christ. **Cyprian**

11

A Pilgrim's Look At Prosperity

*"Lay not up for yourselves treasures upon earth,
where moth and rust doth corrupt." Matt. 6:19*

Do not let it trouble your understanding that we see
the unrighteous with riches while the servants of God
have meager possessions. For if God gave us our reward
right now, we would soon be busying ourselves with
business, not godliness. **2nd Clement**

The Snare Of Prosperity

*"They that will be rich fall into temptation and a snare, and
into many foolish and hurtful lusts, which drown men in
destruction and perdition." 1 Tim. 6:9*

Refrain from much business and you will avoid sin. For
those who are occupied with much business commit many
sins as a result. For they are preoccupied about their
affairs, instead of serving the Lord. How can such a man

who does not serve the Lord ask and receive anything from
the Lord? Those who serve the Lord shall obtain their
requests. But those who do not serve him shall receive
nothing. **Hermas**

Wealth, when not properly governed, is a stronghold
of evil. Many will never reach the kingdom of heaven, for
they have fixed their eyes on wealth. They are sick for the
things of the world. They live proudly through luxury. But
those who are serious about salvation must settle this
beforehand in their minds: All that we possess is given to
us to use for sufficiency, which one may acquire by merely
a few things. The greedy, who take delight in what they
have hoarded, are foolish. It has been said, "He that
gathers wages, gathers into a bag with holes." (Hag. 1:6)
Such is he who gathers corn and shuts it up. He who gives
to no one becomes poorer.

What a farce — what an outright laughable thing it is
— that men bring to banquets urinals made of silver or
crystal. What about the silly rich women who have gold
chamberpots made? Being rich, they cannot even relieve
themselves except in a superb way! I wish that throughout
their whole lives they deemed gold to be fit merely for
dung!

The best riches are poverty of desires. True nobility is
not to be *proud* of wealth, but to *scorn* it. For wisdom is
not bought with the coins of earth. Nor is it sold in the
marketplace. It can only be obtained from heaven. And it
is sold for the true coin, the immortal Logos, the regal gold.
Clement

Love of fine food and love of wine are indeed serious
vices. But they are not as serious as love of luxury. For a

full table and multiple cups are enough to satisfy the gluttonous. But as for those who are fond of gold, purple, and jewels, neither the gold that is above the earth, nor that which is below, is ever sufficient to satisfy them. Even if such a man were to become a Midas, he would not be satisfied. Rather, he would still be poor — craving other people's wealth. Such people are ready to die with their gold. **Clement**

But such people prefer ignorance to wisdom. So they turn their wealth into stones — that is, into pearls and emeralds from India. They squander their wealth on fading dyes, and they throw it away on bought slaves. They are like cooped-up chickens, scraping the dung of life. **Clement**

The Emptiness Of Material Wealth

"A man's life consisteth not in the abundance of the things which he possesseth." Luke 12:15

Iron, brass, and other common substances possess an equality of nature with silver and gold. The origin of both is in the earth. God made things this way to show that the value of gold and silver is no greater than iron and brass. **Tertullian**

Those who are called "rich" add forests to those forests they already own. They exclude the poor from their neighborhoods. They extend their fields far and wide towards the horizon, without limits. They possess immense heaps of silver and gold, along with huge sums of money — either piled in heaps or buried for safekeeping. Yet, in the middle of their riches, they are inwardly torn to pieces by anxiety. Perhaps a robber will steal what they have. Maybe a murderer will attack them. Perhaps, through jealousy, a neighbor with even more wealth will become hostile to them and harass them with vicious lawsuits.

Such a person enjoys no security either in his food or in his sleep. Although he may drink from jeweled goblets, in the middle of the banquet, he frets. And when he lays down his body — all tired from feasting — on his luxurious bed, he lies awake in the midst of the soft feather bed.

Yet, the poor wretch never realizes that his possessions are merely gold-covered torments. He doesn't realize he is held in bondage by his gold. He is not the master of his luxury and wealth — he is their slave! So he goes on obstinately clinging to his tormenting hoards. He is not generous to his dependents, nor does he give anything to the poor.

Such people call their money their own, even though they have to zealously guard it. There it is shut up at home as if it were another's! In the end, neither they, nor their children, nor their friends derive any real benefit from it. Their ownership consists only in this: that they can keep others from possessing it. What a strange trick our language plays on us. People refer to their material possessions as "goods." Yet, they never use it in ways that are good!

Therefore, the one peaceful and trustworthy tranquility — the one solid, firm, and unchanging security — is this: for a man to withdraw from the turbulence of a distracting world. And, anchored in the safe harbor of salvation, to lift his eyes from earth to heaven. He who is actually greater than the world can crave nothing — can desire nothing — from the world. How stable! How free

from all shocks is that safeguard! How heavenly the protection in its unending blessings, to be loosed from the snares of this entangling world, to be purged from earthly dregs, and to be fitted for the light of eternal immortality!
Cyprian

Maybe you haven't noticed, but those who do not know God are rich, powerful and lavished with honors. (1 Tim. 6:9,10) Miserable men! They are lifted up higher merely to fall lower in the end. They're like cattle fattened before the slaughter. (Jas. 5:5) Or the sacrificial animals who are decorated right before they are killed.

Some are given empires and dominions so that their unlimited power will give them the opportunity for the unbridled immorality that is characteristic of ruined souls. Since death is inevitable for everyone, what true happiness can there be apart from the knowledge of God? Like a dream, happiness slips away before it is grasped.

Are you a king? Yet you fear others as much as you are feared. You may be surrounded by abundant followers, yet you are alone in the presence of danger. Are you rich? Yet trusting in wealth is folly. The brief journey of life is not made easier by a large amount of traveling baggage — it's made harder. Do you wear the robes and carry the staff of a magistrate? But what good does it do to glitter in purple and yet be filthy in your mind? It's simply vanity and empty worship of social rank. Are you of noble birth? Do you praise your lineage? Yet we are still all born with one lot. We are distinguished in life only by virtue. (Jas. 2:1-9)
Mark Felix

Simplicity Of Life

*"But godliness with contentment is great gain. For we
brought nothing into this world, and it is certain
we can carry nothing out. And having food and
raiment let us be therewith content."*
1 Tim. 6:6-8

Although there were many prophets of old, they
proclaimed but one God. The inclination to deceive and to
speak falsely belongs to those who covet riches. It belongs
to those who eagerly desire gains. Such an inclination was
far removed from those holy men. For they did not lay up
store for the future. Instead, they carried out the office
entrusted to them in such a manner that they disregarded
all things necessary for the maintenance of life.

They did not even labor for that day's needs, being
content with the unstored food that God had supplied. Not
only did they not have any material gains, they even
endured torments and death. For the ways of righteousness are odious to the wicked. So the prophets, who had
no desire for gain, had neither the inclination nor the
motive to deceive. **Lactantius**

That many of us are called poor is not our disgrace, but
our glory. As our mind is relaxed by luxury, it is strengthened by poverty. Yet who can be poor if he does not want,
if he does not crave the possessions of others? Who can be
poor if he is rich toward God? (Rev. 2:9; Matt. 6:19,20)
Rather, he is poor who, having much, craves still more.

Birds live without any estate. The cattle are fed each
day. Yet these creatures are born for us. We possess all
these things — that is, if we don't lust after them. A
traveler is happier the lighter his load. Likewise, we are

happier on this journey of life when we walk in poverty, rather than groaning under the heavy burden of riches.

Yet, even if we thought that wealth were useful to us, we would ask for it from God. Since all wealth is ultimately his, he could distribute some of it to us if he wanted. But we would rather scorn riches than to strive for them. We would rather possess innocence than wealth. We prefer to ask God for patience rather than for riches. We would rather be good than extravagant. **Mark Felix**

A man is not to labor for wealth of gold or silver. Nor should he own useless implements that are not for some necessary purpose. None of us will make a pickaxe of silver or a sickle of gold, will we? Rather than using materials that are costly, we use materials that are utilitarian.

What prevents us from following the same practice with respect to household utensils? Tell me, does the table knife not cut unless it is studded with silver and its handle is made of ivory? What if the basin is made of earthenware? Will it not receive the dirt of the hands? Will the lamp not give forth light because it is the work of the potter, not of the goldsmith? I know that a trundle bed affords rest just the same as does the ivory couch.

Take note — the Lord ate from a common bowl. He made the disciples recline on the *grass*. He washed their feet, girded with a linen towel — He, the lowly-minded God, the Lord of the universe! He did not bring down a silver footbath from heaven! **Clement**

Let us not interpret covetousness as consisting merely in desiring that which is another's. For even what seems ours is actually another's. For nothing is really ours,

for all things are God's.   And we ourselves are his.
Tertullian

I approve the simplicity of the barbarians. Loving an
unencumbered life, the barbarians have abandoned
luxury. This is what the Lord calls us to be: naked of
luxury, naked of vanity. Having been wrenched from our
sins, we bear the wood of life by itself, aiming only at
salvation. **Clement**

The "Poor In Spirit"

"Blessed are the poor in spirit:
for theirs is the kingdom of heaven."
Matt. 5:3

"Blessed are the poor in spirit." (Matt. 5:3) It is not
simply those who are poor that he pronounces blessed, but
those who have wished to become poor for righteousness'
sake. These are the ones who have scorned the honors of
this world in order to procure that which is truly good.
Clement

Anyone who combines wealth with wrong desires has
mixed a deadly combination. In such a case, to lose the
wealth would be a healthy alternative. To make the soul
pure — that is, poor and bare — we need to focus on the
next words of the Savior, "Come, follow me." (Mark 10:21)
He becomes the way to the pure in heart. God's grace finds
no entrance into the impure soul. And the soul that is rich

in desires, entangled with affection for the things of the world, is impure.

Yet, some people are able to hold their gold, silver, houses, and other possessions simply as the gifts of God. They use their things to minister for the salvation of men. They thereby return them to God, who gave them. They know that they possess them more for the sake of their brothers than for themselves. They are the *masters* of their belongings, not the *slaves* of their belongings. They don't carry their possessions around in their *soul,* nor do they plan their life around their things. Instead, they are always laboring at some good, divinely-inspired activity.

Even if they sometimes need to be deprived of their things, they are able to cheerfully bear the removal of their belongings just as easily as they were able to enjoy their abundance. (Phil. 4:11,12) These are the ones who are blessed by the Lord. They are the ones he calls "poor *in spirit.*" (Matt. 5:3) They are the proper heirs of the kingdom of heaven.

But there are others who carry their riches in their souls. Instead of being filled with God's Spirit, their hearts are filled with their gold or their land. They are always acquiring possessions, and they are perpetually on the lookout for more. They are bent down and fettered to the toils of the world. They are of the earth and destined to become a part of the earth. How can they desire or pay attention to the kingdom of heaven? They don't carry around *hearts* in their bodies. Instead, they carry around land or precious metals. You'll always find them in the midst of the objects they have chosen. For where the mind of man is, there also is his treasure. (Matt. 6:21) **Clement**

12

The Godly Use Of Wealth

"If therefore you have not been faithful
in the use of unrighteous mammon,
who will entrust the true riches to you?"
Luke 16:11 NAS

He who is rich has much material wealth. But such a man is poor in matters relating to the Lord, because he is distracted by his riches. As a result, he offers very few confessions and intercessions to the Lord. Those that he does offer are small and weak, and have no power above. However, when the rich man aids the poor man, helping him with his needs, then the poor man, being helped by the rich, intercedes for him, giving thanks to God for the man who has bestowed gifts upon him. For the poor man is rich in intercession and confession. And his intercession has great power with God. (Luke 16:9) **Hermas**

But what if someone is able, although in the midst of wealth, to turn away from its power? What if he is still able to maintain moderation in his feelings and to exercise self-control? What if he is able to seek God alone — to breathe God and walk with God? Then such a man is really poor. He submits to God's commandments and he is unconquered and unharmed by wealth. He lives free of its disease. But if that's not the case, then "it will be easier for a camel to go through a needle's eye, than for such a rich man to reach the kingdom of God." (Mark 10:25) **Clement**

Jesus said, "Make friends with the wealth of unrighteousness, so that when you fail, they may receive you into eternal homes." (Luke 16:9) When he said this, he showed that by its nature, all property that a man possesses by his own power is not really his own. And from this unrighteousness [i.e. wealth], we are allowed to perform a righteous and saving thing — to refresh those who have an eternal dwelling with the Father.

Notice that he has not told you to wait until someone asks or begs you to share your wealth. No. You yourself must look for those worthy disciples of the Savior whom you can aid. As the apostle has most excellently put it, "The Lord loves a cheerful giver." (2 Cor. 9:7) The cheerful giver delights in giving. He doesn't hold anything back. Instead, he sows so that he will reap. He does it without murmuring, disputing, or showing regret. This is giving that is pure. Even more blessed is what the Lord said in another place: "Give to everyone who asks you." (Luke 6:30) This shows how delighted God is when we give. And this saying is above all divinity: not waiting to be asked, but finding out for ourselves who deserve to receive kindness. **Clement**

Although adopting parrots and curlews, people of the world do not adopt orphan children. Instead, they abandon their young babies born at home, leaving them to die. Yet, they adopt the young of the birds. So they prefer irrational

creatures to those who are rational. Instead, they should
take care of the elderly. For the elderly are certainly fairer
in mind than pet apes, and they can utter things that are
better than what nightingales chirp. Such people should
consider the sayings, "He that pities the poor lends to the
Lord," (Pro. 19:17) and "Inasmuch as you have done it to
the least of these my brothers, you have done it to me."
(Matt. 25:40) **Clement**

God caused the human race to share together by first
giving that which was His own: His own Logos [i.e. his
Son]. The Logos was given to be owned commonly by all.
And God made all things for everyone. All things are
therefore to be owned in common, and not for the rich to
hoard an undue share. Some say, "I possess, and possess
in abundance. Why then should I not enjoy?" But that
saying is suitable neither to the individual nor to society
at large. It is more worthy of love to say, "I have, so why
should I not give to those who need?" I well understand
that God has given to us the freedom to use our possessions. But this freedom applies only to the extent of what
is necessary. And God has determined that we should
share what we have. For it is monstrous for one person to
live in luxury, while many others are in want. **Clement**

To become upset at all monetary losses is the business
of Gentiles, not Christians. For Gentiles give precedence
to money over their own souls. They risk their lives at sea
simply for the gain of money. They hire themselves out for
sport and for war. Some of them even act like wild beasts,
becoming bandits along the highway. But we are distinguished from them by our separation. Rather than laying
down our souls for money, we lay down our money for our

souls. That is, we endure it patiently when our money is taken from us, and we spontaneously give our money to those in need. **Tertullian**

The Rich Man Who Said "Yes"

"And when he was gone forth into the way, there came one running, and kneeled to him, and asked him, Good Master, what shall I do that I may inherit eternal life? ... Then Jesus beholding him loved him, and said unto him, One thing thou lackest: go thy way, sell whatsoever thou hast, and give to the poor, and thou shalt have treasure in heaven: and come, take up the cross, and follow me." Mark 10:17,21

Cyprian was born around the year 200 to a noble and wealthy pagan family in Carthage, North Africa. Before coming to know Christ, he lived in worldly splendor and became a renowned teacher of rhetoric. Yet, upon discovering the true riches of Christ, he literally followed Jesus' words above, and he gave all of his property to the poor and became a servant of Christ. He labored diligently on behalf of the church in Carthage and eventually died as a martyr for his Lord and Savior. Here are some of his insights about material wealth.

With what rewards does the Lord invite us to scorn worldly wealth? With what compensations does he make up for the small and trifling losses we suffer in this present age? He says, "There is no man that leaves house, land, parents, brothers, wife, or children for the kingdom of God's sake but he shall receive a hundredfold even in this life, but in the world to come, life everlasting." (Mark 10:29,30) If we know these things — if we have experienced them from the truth of the Lord who promises — we do not fear the loss of our material possessions. In fact, we *desire* their loss.

"If, therefore, you have not been faithful in unrighteous mammon, who will entrust the *true* to you? And if you have not been faithful in that which is another's, who will give you that which is your own?" (Luke 16:11,12) Are you afraid that if you give generously, your estate will be exhausted as a result? That you may be reduced to poverty? If so, have righteous courage in this respect. Be free from care. That which is supplied by the work of Christ cannot be exhausted.

Are you afraid that perhaps your estate will die away if you give generously from it? Don't you know, miserable man, that while you are fearing for your estate, life itself and salvation are dying away! While you are anxious lest your wealth should be diminished, you yourself are being diminished.

God feeds the birds. He gives daily food to the sparrows. There is no lack of food and drink to creatures that have no sense of divine things. So do you think that *anything* will be lacking to a Christian — to a servant of the Lord, to one given up to good works, to one who is dear to his Lord?

Do you really imagine that earthly things will be lacking to those to whom heavenly and divine things are given? Where does this unbelieving thought — this impious and unholy belief — come from? What is a faithless heart doing in a home of faith? Why is a person who does not completely trust in Christ even called a Christian? The name of "Pharisee" is more fitting for such a person!

You are the captive and slave of your money! You are fettered with the chains and ropes of covetousness. Christ freed you, but you are once more back in chains. You keep your money, but your money will be unable to keep you. "You fool! This night your soul is required of you; and who will own what you have prepared?" (Luke 12:20) Why do you watch in loneliness over your riches? Why do you store up the burden of your estate for your own punishment — that in proportion to your riches in this world, you may become poor to God?

Divide your profits with the Lord your God. Share your gains with Christ. Make Christ a partner with you in your earthly possessions, so that he also may make you a fellow-heir with him in his heavenly kingdom. The state cannot take away the property entrusted to God. Neither can the tax collector intrude on it. Such an inheritance is placed in security that is kept under the guardianship of God.

You are an unfair and traitorous father unless you faithfully show concern for your children — that is, unless you plan ahead to help preserve them in religion and true devotion. Otherwise, you are leaving your children in the care of the devil rather than that of Christ. You are sinning doubly when you teach your children to love their property more than Christ.

What more could Christ have done to stimulate us to works of righteousness and mercy than to say that whatever is given to the needy and the poor is given to himself? By saying that he is grieved unless the needy and poor are provided for? In this manner, if someone in the church is not motivated out of consideration for his brother, perhaps he will be moved out of concern for Christ.

So let us give earthly garments to Christ that we may receive heavenly clothing. Let us give food and drink of this world that we may come with Abraham, Isaac, and Jacob to the heavenly banquet.

And let us remember, beloved brethren, what the congregation of believers did in the days of the apostles, when at the very beginning, their hearts flourished with greater virtues. At that time, the faith of believers burned with a warmth of faith that was new. They sold houses and farms, and they joyfully and generously presented the

proceeds to the apostles to be distributed to the poor. By
selling and alienating their earthly estates, they trans-
ferred their lands to the place where they might receive
the fruits of an eternal possession.

As we read in the Acts of the Apostles: "And the
congregation of those who believed acted with one heart
and soul. Neither was there any distinction among them,
nor did they claim that anything belonging to them was
their own. Rather, they had all things in common." (Acts
4:32) This is truly to become sons of God by spiritual birth.
This is to imitate the fairness of God the Father by the
heavenly law. For whatever is from God is available for all
to use in common. And no one is excluded from His benefits
and gifts. **Cyprian**

Advice To An Emperor

The following is an excerpt from another one of the essays of
Lactantius written to the Emperor Constantine, instructing him in
the ways of Christianity — in contrast to the wisdom of the world.

The primary and best benefit of riches is this: Not to
use wealth for the pleasure of one individual, but to use it
for the benefit of many. Use it, not for one's own personal
enjoyment, but for justice — because justice does not
perish. The hope of receiving something in return must be
altogether absent from the responsibility of showing
mercy. The reward for mercy must come from God alone.
For if you expect a reward back from the one you help, then
that is not kindness. It is simply loaning some benefit to
another with interest.

Yet, the wonderful thing in this is that whenever a
man gives to another without thought of return, he really
gives to himself. For he will receive a reward from God.

Cicero said, "Hospitality is rightly praised. For it is quite fitting that the houses of illustrious men should be open to illustrious guests." But Cicero was in error. The house of the just and wise man should *not* be open to the illustrious. Rather, it should be open to the lowly and wretched. For God has commanded that when we give a feast, we should invite those who cannot invite us back in return.

The ransoming of captives is a great and noble exercise of justice. Yet, he who does good only to a neighbor, friend, or relative, certainly deserves no great praise, for he is bound to do such. He would be unrighteous and detestable if he did not do that which both nature and kinship requires. But he who ransoms a stranger — a person unknown to him — is truly worthy of praise. For he is led to do it by kindness only. So justice exists where there is no obligation or necessity of conferring a benefit.

And it is no less a great work of justice to protect and defend orphans and widows who are destitute and who stand in need of assistance. Accordingly, the divine law prescribes this to all. And one reason why God commands that widows and orphans should be defended and cherished is this: that no one should refrain from dying a martyr's death because of concern for the welfare of his dependents. Rather, he can face death with promptness and boldness. For he knows that he leaves his loved ones to the care of God and that they will never lack provisions.

Another great kindness is to assist and support those who are sick and need someone to aid them. The last and greatest office of godliness is to bury strangers and the poor. For we should not allow the image and workmanship of God to lie exposed as prey for animals and birds. Rather, we should restore it to the earth, from which it came.
Lactantius

How Wealth Can Cost Christians Their Eternal Life

"It is easier for a camel to go through the eye of a needle, than for a rich man to enter into the kingdom of God."
Matt. 19:24

During the second and third centuries, it was a capital crime to be a Christian. Tens of thousands of Christians were imprisoned, tortured, and slain. So one of the mildest forms of persecution was simply to have one's property confiscated by the state. This latter form of persecution was an easy matter for impoverished Christians to endure, but an extreme trial for wealthy Christians. As a result, many wealthy Christians denied Christ when persecution broke out.

You know that you who are the servants of God dwell in a strange land. For your city is far away from this one. If then you recognize your city in which you are to dwell, why do you acquire lands here? Why do you make expensive preparations and accumulate houses and useless buildings? He who makes such preparations for this earthly city cannot return again to his own city. Do you not understand that all these things belong to another? Do you not know that they are under the power of another?

For the lord of this earthly city will say, "I don't want you to dwell in my city any longer. So depart from this city, for you do not obey my laws." Having acquired fields, houses, and many other things, what are you going to do? When the ruler casts you out, what will you do with your land, your house, and your other possessions that you gathered to yourself? For the lord of this earthly country justly says to you, "Either obey my laws or depart from my kingdom." What then will you do, you who have a law in your own city? Will you be able to deny your law because of your land or your other possessions? Take heed lest it works to your ruin!

For if you shall desire to return to your own city, you will not be received. For you have denied the law of your city. So you will be excluded from it. Walk carefully, then, as one living in a foreign land. Make no further preparations for yourself than what is merely sufficient. And when the master of this city will come and cast you out for disobeying his law, be ready to leave this earthly city and to depart to your own. Be ready to obey your own law without being subjected to grief. Instead, be ready to obey with great joy.

You, then, who serve the Lord, be on watch! Have him in your hearts, that you may do the works of God, remembering his commandments and his promises. Believe that he will bring those promises to pass if his commandments are observed. So instead of buying lands, buy needy souls, to the extent you are able. Visit widows and orphans and take care not to overlook them. Spend your wealth and all your possessions that you have received from the Lord on such "lands" and "houses" as these. **Hermas**

13

The New Birth

*"Verily, verily, I say unto thee, Except a man be born again,
he cannot see the kingdom of God." John 3:3*

I used to regard it as a difficult matter — particularly
in light of my character at that time — that a man could
be capable of being born again. Yet, this was a truth that
the divine mercy had announced for my salvation. I used
to doubt that a man who had been quickened to a new life
in the bath of saving water could be able to put aside what
he had previously been. I questioned whether a person
could be changed in heart and soul while still retaining all
of his bodily structure.

I said, "How could such a conversion be possible — that
there should be a sudden and rapid putting aside of all
those things which are innate in us and have become
hardened in the corruption of our physical nature? Or, to
put aside those traits we have acquired and which have
become deep-rooted in us? These things are all deeply and
thoroughly ingrained in us. How does the person who has
been used to expensive banquets and sumptuous feasts
learn to enjoy simplicity? Or, the person who has glittered
in gold and purple and has been celebrated for his
expensive clothes — how can he reduce himself to ordinary
and simple clothing?

"How can the one who has experienced the power of rulership and the charm of civic honors help but to shrink from the thought of becoming a mere private and unknown citizen? It has always been true that the love of wine entices humans. Pride puffs us up. Anger inflames us. We are discontented because of covetousness. Cruelty excites us. Ambition delights us. And lust hastens us to ruin. These things are inevitable, and these allurements will never let go of the person they bind!"

Yes, those were my frequent thoughts. Through the innumerable errors of my former life, I was held in bondage. And I did not believe that I could possibly be delivered from this bondage. As a result, I gave in to my various clinging vices. And because I had no hope of anything better, I used to indulge my sins as though they were actually parts of me — native to me.

However, after that, by the help of the water of new birth, the stain of former years was washed away. (Acts 2:38) And a light from above, serene and pure was infused into my reconciled heart. And then, by the agency of the Spirit that was breathed down from heaven, a second birth had restored me to a new man. Thereafter, in a wondrous manner, doubtful things soon began to assure themselves to me. Hidden things became revealed. Dark things were enlightened. What I had formerly thought impossible, now was capable of being achieved.

In short, I was enabled to see that my former life, born of the flesh, was a life of practicing sin. It was of the earth — earthly. But my life had now begun to be of God, and it was enlivened by the Spirit of holiness. Of this change, I cannot boast, but can only be grateful. We do not ascribe this to man's virtue, but declare it to be the gift of God. So now the beginning of the work of faith is that we no longer practice sin. The fact that we used to sin was the result of human error — not God. All of our power is of God. I repeat, of God. From him we have life. From him we have strength. While yet in this world, by his power, we foreknow the indications of things to come.

However, let fear be the keeper of our innocence, so that the assurance we have gained may not give birth to carelessness, and the old enemy end up creeping up on us again. Therefore, let us, through righteous submissiveness, keep the Lord in the chambers of a grateful mind, for out of his mercy he has flowed into our hearts through celestial grace. **Cyprian**

God allows us to know and condemn what we used to be so that we will have more love for what we *shall* be. Yet, we do not have to purchase these things with either money or labor. A man's elevation from his previous life and his new power is not begotten in him through elaborate effort. Rather, it is a free gift from God. And it is accessible to all. Just as the sun shines spontaneously on all, just as the day gives light, just as the fountains flow, just as the rain gives moisture — so does the heavenly Spirit infuse itself into us. When the soul, in its gaze into heaven, recognizes its Author, it rises higher than the sun. It far transcends all this earthly power and begins to be that which it was meant to be. **Cyprian**

It is a source of joy and glory to men to have children who are like themselves. How much greater is the joy of God the Father when anyone is so spiritually born that in his actions and in the praises of his lips, he announces his noble birth from God. **Cyprian**

14

Counsel To Church Leaders

"If a man aspires to the office of overseer,
it is a fine work he desires to do."
1 Tim. 3:1 NAS

Be An Example In Simple Living

"An overseer, then, must be ... free from the love of money."
1 Tim. 3:3 NAS

A bishop [overseer] should be content with merely enough food and provisions as suits necessity and propriety. He should not use the Lord's goods as though they were another's. Rather, he should use them moderately. "For the worker is worthy of his reward." (Luke 10:7) He should not be indulgent in diet nor fond of idle furniture. Rather, he should be content with merely that which is sufficient for his sustenance. **Constitutions of the Holy Apostles**

On Being A Loving Shepherd

"He said to him, 'Shepherd My sheep.'" John 21:16 NAS

When any Christian becomes an orphan, whether it be
a young man or a maiden, it is good for one of the brethren
who is without a child to take the young man or woman
and cherish him or her as his own child. And he that has
a son about the same age as the orphan maiden, and who
is marriageable, should marry the maiden to the son. For
they who do so do a great work and become fathers to the
orphans.

Therefore, you bishops should be attentive to the care
of those in need, lacking in nothing towards them. To
orphans, you should give the same care that parents would
give. To the widows, you should give the care of a husband.
To those of suitable age, you should help them to get
married. To the workman, you should provide work. To
those unable to work, compassion. To strangers, a house.
To the hungry, food. To the thirsty, something to drink.
To the naked, clothing. To the sick, visitation. To the
prisoners, assistance.

And you should have greater care for the orphans, so
that they may lack nothing. You must provide for the
orphan maiden until she arrives at the age of marriage.
And then you should give her in marriage to a brother.

To the young man, give assistance that he may learn
a trade and may be maintained thereby. And when he has
mastered a trade, he will be able to buy himself the
necessary tools of his trade. In that manner, he will no
longer be a burden to any of the brethren, who have a
sincere love for him. Rather, he will be able to support
himself. As a result, he will not consume the provisions
needed for the orphan, the stranger, or the widow.

However, he that receives assistance in hypocrisy or as a result of idleness — instead of working and helping others — is obnoxious before God and is deserving of God's punishment. For he has snatched away the morsel from the one who is truly needy.

We exhort the widows and orphans to partake of the things that are given to them with all fear and godly reverence. And they should return thanks to God who gives food to the needy. **Constitutions of the Holy Apostles**

Practice What You Preach!

"Nor yet as lording it over those allotted to your charge, but proving to be examples to the flock."
1 Pet. 5:3

As to anyone who teaches principles to live by and molds the character of others, I ask, "Is he not obligated himself to live by the principles he teaches?" If he himself does not live by them, his teaching is nullified. His student will answer him like this, "I cannot practice the things you teach, because they are impossible. You forbid me to be angry. You forbid me to covet. You forbid me to lust. And you forbid me to fear pain and death. This is totally contrary to nature; all living creatures are subject to these emotions. If you are so convinced that it is possible to live contrary to natural impulses, first let me see you practice the things you teach so I will know they are possible."

How will the teacher take away this excuse from the self-willed, unless he teaches them by his *deeds*, so they can see with their own eyes that the things he teaches are possible. For this very reason, no one obeys the teachings

of the philosophers. Men prefer examples to words,
because it is easy to speak — but difficult to act.
Lactantius

If a person renders any Christian service for the sake
of payment, is he not bound by the customs of this world?
He is like a hired man who has done well and now comes
running to receive his payment. In contrast, we should
imitate the Lord to the extent we are able. And we imitate
him when we comply with the will of God, receiving
without cost and giving without cost. We thereby receive
citizenship [in the Kingdom] as a worthy reward in itself.
Clement

PART

TWO

15

Pilgrim Meditations

When false witnesses testified against our Lord and Savior Jesus Christ, he remained silent. And when unfounded charges were brought against him, he gave no answer. For he believed that his whole life and his conduct among the Jews were a better refutation than any verbal answer to the false testimony.

And yet even now he continues silent before his accusers. He makes no audible answer. Rather, he places his defense in the lives of his genuine disciples. For they are a pre-eminent testimony — one that rises above all false witness. They refute and overthrow all unfounded accusations and charges. **Origen**

Who would any longer call what is constantly spoken of by people noble birth in its true sense, once he has known the noble birth of the sons of God? And how will the mind that has contemplated the unshakable kingdom of Christ (cf. Heb. 12:28) fail to despise as worth nothing every kingdom on earth? **Origen**[1]

There are two kinds of fear. The first kind is fear
accompanied with reverence. This is the type of fear that
citizens show towards good rulers. Right-minded children
have this type of fear for their fathers. And we have this
type of fear for God. The second kind is fear accompanied
with hatred. This is the sort of fear that slaves feel towards
masters that are harsh. The Hebrews had this sort of fear
of God, for they made God a master, not a father.
Clement

Having the truth itself as our rule, and having the
testimony about God set clearly before us, we should not
cast away this firm and true knowledge of God by running
after numerous diverse questions. **Irenaeus**

We should not accept the word of salvation simply
because of fear of punishment or because of the promised
reward. Rather, we should accept it on account of its
inherent good. **Clement**

"Blessed are the meek, for they shall inherit the earth."
(Matt. 5:5) And the meek are those who have quelled the
battle of unbelief in the soul, the battle of wrath and lust,
and the other battles waged inside of them. **Clement**

Doesn't he who denies the Lord really deny himself?
For by depriving himself of his relationship to the Lord,
he does not rob his Master of His authority. So he who
denies the Savior denies life. For "the Light was life."
(John 1:4) **Clement**

In a sense, the world resembles the sea. Now, the sea would have long ago dried up by reason of its saltiness if it were not for the constant inflow of the rivers and springs that supply it. Likewise, if the world had not had the law of God and the prophets, who flowed and gushed forth sweetness, compassion, and righteousness, and who taught the holy commandments of God, it would have long ago come to ruin. For wickedness and sin abound in it.

Also, in the sea there are islands. Some of them are inhabitable, well-watered, and fruitful. They have havens and harbors, in which the storm-tossed travelers may find refuge. Likewise, this world is driven and storm-tossed by sins. So God has given it assemblies, that is, the holy churches. The doctrines of truth survive in these churches, as though securely anchored in an island harbor. And those who desire to be saved, being lovers of truth, run into these islands, wishing to escape the wrath and judgment of God.

However, other islands are rocky and without water. They are barren, infested with wild beasts and are uninhabitable. They serve only to injure navigators and storm-tossed travelers. In fact ships are wrecked on them, and those driven to them perish. Similarly, there are heresies — doctrines of error that destroy those who approach them. For they are not guided by the word of truth. **Theophilus**

Since we draw up wills for worldly matters, how much more so should we plan for our posterity in things that are divine and heavenly! We thereby, in a sense, bequeath a legacy that will be received before the material inheritance is divided. The legacy I am speaking of is one of admonition and example. **Tertullian**

God's resting does not mean, as some conceive, that
God ceased from doing anything. For, being good, if he
should ever cease from doing good, then he would cease
from being God. **Clement**

"One of the soldiers with a spear pierced his side, and
there came from it blood and water. And he that saw it
bore record, and his record is true, and he knows that he
says the truth." (John 19:34,35) Now, in other dead bodies,
the blood congeals. Pure water does not flow forth. But the
miraculous feature in the case of the dead body of Jesus
was that blood and *water* flowed from his side. **Origen**

The voice from the cloud on the high mountain was
heard only by those who had gone up with Christ. For the
divine voice is of such a nature, as to be heard only by those
whom the Speaker wishes to hear it. Therefore, I maintain
that the voice of God is not air in motion that has been
struck. Nor is it any vibration of air. Nor is it anything else
that is mentioned in treatises on the human voice. **Origen**

Because he is not known by wicked men, God desires
to make himself known to them. He does not do this
because he feels deprived of their worship. Rather, he
makes himself known because the knowledge of him will
free the wicked from their unhappiness. **Origen**

Civil law is one thing, and it varies everywhere
according to customs. But justice is another thing, which
God has set forth to all in a uniform and uncomplicated

manner. And he who is ignorant of God is of necessity ignorant about justice.

But let us suppose that it would be possible for one to gain true virtue merely by natural and innate goodness. We have heard that Cimon of Athens was this sort of man. He gave alms to the needy, took care of the poor, and clothed the naked. Yet, when that one thing is lacking that is of the greatest importance — the acknowledgment of God — then all those good things are superfluous and empty. In pursuing them, he has labored in vain. For his justice will resemble a human body that has no head.

Therefore, the sum and substance of everything is contained in the acknowledgment and worship of God. All of the hope and safety of man centers on this. This is the first step of wisdom: to know who is our true Father, to worship him with the holiness that is due to him, to obey him, and to yield ourselves to his service with the utmost devotion. **Lactantius**

He is not of sound mind, who, without having any greater hope set before him except this life, prefers labors, tortures, and miseries to those things that others enjoy in life. **Lactantius**

"Render Caesar's things unto Caesar and God's things unto God." What are Caesar's things? Those things that bear the image of Caesar, such as the denarius. And what are the things that are God's? Man himself, who has been stamped with God's image and name. **Tertullian**

The greatest of orators have often been overcome by speakers of only moderate ability. For the power of truth

is so great that it defends itself even in small things by its
own clarity. **Lactantius**

Those who have devoted themselves to the Father have
proved to be good fathers to their children. Those who have
known the Son are good parents to their sons. Those who
remember the Bridegroom are good husbands to their
wives. Finally, those who have been redeemed from utter
slavery are good masters to their servants. **Clement**

Whatever you are to believe about God, you must learn
it from God himself. If you do not obtain this knowledge
from God, you will be unable to obtain it from any other
person. For who is able to reveal that which God has
hidden? **Tertullian**

The Folly Of Human Wisdom

"The wisdom of this world is foolishness with God."
1 Cor. 3:19

Those of us who have adopted the true life have abandoned luxury as something ensnaring and unnecessary.
However, in its place, we must cultivate *more* than a
simple way of life. We must also cultivate a modest style
of speech, one that is not showy and lofty. For "the wisdom
of the world is foolishness with God," and "The Lord knows
the reasonings of the wise, that they are foolish." (1 Cor.
3:19,20) Let no one glory, therefore, because of his pre-
eminence in human learning. **Clement**

As I have often said before, I have neither practiced nor studied to express myself in pure Greek. Such study suits those who seduce the multitudes away from the truth. In my opinion, he who is seeking truth should not frame his thoughts in language that is learned and refined. He should merely aim at expressing his meaning as best he can. For those who are fussy about words, and devote their time to studying grammar, miss the significance of things. **Clement**

The truth — that is, the secret of the Most High God, who created all things — cannot be obtained by our own ability and perceptions. If human thought could reach to the counsels and affairs of that Eternal Majesty, there would be no difference between God and man.

And because it was impossible that the divine methods should become known to man by man's own efforts, God did not permit man to err any longer in his search for the light of wisdom. God did not want man to continue to fruitlessly wander through impenetrable darkness. So at length, God opened man's eyes. He made man's investigation of the truth His own gift. Thereby He can show the emptiness of human wisdom. **Lactantius**

Wise men have attacked false religions. For they perceived their falsehood. But they were unable to introduce *true* religion because they did not know what it was or where it could be found. In that they understood the error of false religion, they proved themselves superior in wisdom. Yet, they also rendered themselves so much the more foolish, for they did not imagine that *any* religion was true.

So philosophers have reached the height of *human* wisdom in that they understand that which is not true.

But they have failed in being able to say what really is true. It is a well-known saying of Cicero, "I wish that I could as easily find out what *is* true as I can refute those things that are not." **Lactantius**

The important thing is the truth of the argument, not the authority of the speaker. In fact, the more unpretentious the discourse, the more evident the reasoning. For it isn't colored by the pomp of eloquence and grace; it is sustained by its own truth. **Mark Felix**

The Unity Of The Church

"Neither pray I for these alone, but for them also which shall believe on me through their word; That they all may be one."
John 17:20,21

You cannot separate a ray of the sun from its body of light, for you will find that its unity does not allow the stream of light to be broken. Break a branch from a tree; when broken, it will not be able to bud. Cut a stream off from its spring, and that which is cut off will dry up. Likewise, the Church, arrayed with the light of the Lord, sheds forth her rays over the whole world. Yet, it is one light that is everywhere radiated. The unity of the body is not separated. **Cyprian**

---

[1]Origen, *Origen*, trans. and ed. Rowan A. Greer (New York: Paulist Press, 1979), p. 117. Copyright © 1979 by The Missionary Society of St. Paul the Apostle in the State of New York. Used by permission.

16

Brotherly Compassion

"Then shall the King say unto them on his right hand, Come, ye blessed of my Father, inherit the kingdom prepared for you from the foundation of the world: For I was a hungered, and ye gave me meat: I was thirsty, and ye gave me drink: I was a stranger, and ye took me in: Naked, and ye clothed me: I was sick, and ye visited me: I was in prison, and ye came unto me."
Matt. 25:34-36

Around the year 250, a band of marauding barbarians swept through Numidia in northern Africa, taking much of the population captive and holding them for ransom. Among those captured were a number of Christians. As the remaining Christians in Numidia did not have sufficient funds to ransom these captives, they wrote Cyprian, the bishop in the nearby city of Carthage, to see if his congregation could help. Here is his letter of reply:

Cyprian to Januarius, Maximus, and Victor, his brothers: Greetings. With extreme grief of mind, and with tears, dearest brothers, I have read your letter that you wrote to me out of loving care about the captivity of our brothers and sisters there. For who would not grieve over such things! Who would not consider his brother's grief his own. For the Apostle Paul spoke, saying, "When one member suffers, all the members suffer with him. Or when one member rejoices, all the members rejoice with him." (1 Cor. 12:26)

113

Accordingly, the captivity of our brothers must be considered as our *own* captivity. The grief of those who are endangered must be viewed as our own grief. For there is but one body of our union. So both love and the duties of religion should strengthen us and prompt us to redeem these brothers and sisters.

Furthermore, the Apostle Paul says, "Do you not know that you are the temple of God and that the Spirit of God dwells in you?" (1 Cor. 3:16) So in effect it is temples of God that have been taken captive. And we should not allow the temples of God to be captive for long, due to any slothfulness or neglect on our part. Rather, we should strive with what powers we have to act quickly and by our obedience to deserve well of Christ our Judge and Lord and God.

Moreover, the Apostle Paul says, "As many of you as have been baptized into Christ have put on Christ." (Gal. 3:27) Christ is to be seen in our captive brothers, and he who redeemed us from death is to be redeemed from the peril of captivity. Christ allows these things to happen so that our faith may be tested. He wants to see whether each one of us will do for another what he would wish to be done for Him if He were held captive by barbarians.

What father would not consider it as though his own sons are captive there, out of mutual love. Or what husband would not view it as though his own wife were held captive there? But how great is the general grief and suffering among all of us concerning the peril of the virgins who have been captured. On their behalf, we not only bewail their loss of *liberty*, but also their loss of *modesty*. We lament the chains of the barbarians less than the violence of seducers and abominable places. We fear that those sisters dedicated to Christ and devoted forever in honor of singleness by modest virtue, should be sullied by the lust and poison of the Accuser.

After considering all of these things and sorrowfully examining all of the matters you spoke of in your letter, our brothers have all promptly, willingly, and generously gathered sums of money for the captured brothers and sisters. For these brethren have always been prone to do the work of God according to the strength of their faith. But now they are even stirred on to even more godly works after considering so great an amount of suffering. For the Lord says in his Gospel, "I was sick, and you visited me." (Matt. 25:36) How much more will he say, "I lay captive and chained among barbarians, and from that prison of slavery, you delivered me."

Finally, we give you warmest thanks that you wished us to be sharers in your sorrow and in this great and necessary work. We thank you for offering us fruitful fields in which we could sow the seeds of our hope, with the expectation of a harvest of the most abundant fruits that will proceed from this heavenly and saving mission. Accordingly, we have sent you a sum of one hundred thousand sestertia* that has been collected here in the church over which we preside by the Lord's mercy.

We wish, indeed, that nothing of this kind ever happens again and that our brothers, protected by the Lord's majesty, may be safely preserved from perils of this kind. However, perhaps this type of thing will happen again in order for God to search out the love of our minds and to test the faith of our hearts. If so, do not delay to tell us of it in your letters. For you can be assured that our church and the whole brotherhood here earnestly pray that these things will never happen again. But if they do happen, be assured that we will willingly and generously render help again.

Dearest brothers, we heartily bid you farewell. Please remember us.

---

*a sestertius was equal to one-fourth of a denarius, a day's wage. A laborer would have had to work over 80 years to earn 100,000 sestertia. Based on the earnings of the average American wage earner today, this sum would be equivalent to over 1.6 million dollars.

17

Scripture:
The Pilgrim's Guidepost

*"Thy word is a lamp unto my feet,
and a light unto my path."*
Ps. 119:105

The blessed apostle Paul wrote to no more than seven churches by name, in this order: the first to the Corinthians, the second to the Ephesians, the third to the Philippians, the fourth to the Colossians, the fifth to the Galatians, the sixth to the Thessalonians, and the seventh to the Romans. (He wrote to the Corinthians and Thessalonians twice for their correction.) By this sevenfold writing, it shows that there is one Church spread abroad throughout the whole world. Likewise, John, who wrote only to seven churches in the Apocalypse, actually addressed *all* churches. **Caius**

The Inspiration Of Scripture

*"All Scripture is given by inspiration of God, and is
profitable for doctrine, for reproof, for correction, for
instruction in righteousness." 2 Tim. 3:16*

When we demonstrate the deity of Christ by making
use of the prophetic declarations regarding him, we also
demonstrate that the writings which prophesied of him
were divinely inspired. And we must also say that the
divinity of the prophetic declarations, and of the spiritual
nature of the Law of Moses, shone forth after the coming
of Christ. For before the coming of Christ, it was not totally
possible to bring forth clear proofs of the divine inspiration
of the ancient Scriptures. However, his coming clearly
convicted those who had suspected that the Law and
prophets were not divine; it demonstrated to them that
Scripture was written by heavenly grace.

Just by reading the words of the prophets with care
and attention, the reader will feel the traces of divinity
that are in them. Such a reader will be led by his inner
emotions to believe that those words that have been
deemed to be the words of God are not the works of men.
Moreover, the light that was contained in the law of Moses,
but which had been concealed by a veil, shone forth at the
coming of Jesus. The veil was taken away. And those
blessings, the shadow of which was contained in the letter,
came forth gradually to the knowledge of men.

Yet, it is nothing to be surprised about when the
superhuman element of thought in Scripture is not
immediately grasped by the novice. The Providence of God
that embraces the whole world is similar. It is clear to
everyone that certain things are the works of Providence.
However, other aspects of God's care are concealed. As a
result, some people disbelieve that God orders all things

with unspeakable skill and power. For the artistic plan of a providential Ruler is not so evident in some matters.

Yet, to those who believe, the doctrine of Providence is not at all weakened on account of those things that are not understood. Likewise, neither is the divinity of Scripture — which extends to *all* Scripture — lost on account of our weak inability to discover in *every* passage the hidden splendor of those doctrines that are veiled in common and unattractive phraseology. **Origen**

The Humble Diction Of Scripture

"Now as they observed the confidence of Peter and John, and understood that they were uneducated and untrained men, they were marveling." Acts 4:13 NAS

The New Testament Scriptures were written in *koine* Greek — the unpolished street language of the eastern Roman empire. As a result, educated Romans often scoffed at the Christian Scriptures. But this humble diction is no reason to discredit Scripture. Rather, as the early Christians pointed out, to present profound truths in unpretentious language is something quite marvelous.

You say that our writings [i.e. Scripture] were written by unlearned and ignorant men and that they therefore should not be believed. Actually, this provides a stronger reason to believe that they have not been adulterated by false statements. They were written by men of simple mind, who did not know how to cunningly devise tales with alluring ornaments. Instead, their language is ordinary and humble. For truth never seeks deceitful polish. **Arnobius**

The fault, I suppose, of the divine teachings lie in the fact that they sprang from Judea instead of Greece! Apparently, Christ made a mistake, too, in sending out fishermen to preach instead of philosophers! **Tertullian**

Simple and undisguised truth should be more clear, for it has sufficient ornament of itself. For this reason, it is corrupted when it is embellished with external adornments. In contrast, falsehood is made more pleasing by added splendor. Since falsehood is recognized as being corrupt when it stands alone, it vanishes and dissipates unless it is embellished and polished with external adornment. **Lactantius**

When educated men study the religion of God, they refuse to believe unless they are instructed by some skillful teacher. For being accustomed to sweet and polished speeches or poems, they disdain the simple and common language of the sacred writings, viewing them as inferior. For they seek that which soothes the senses.

But is God, the Maker of the mind, the voice, and the tongue, unable to speak eloquently? Of course not! Rather, with the greatest of foresight, he desired that divine truths be presented without adornment. In that way, *all* persons can understand the things which he himself has spoken to all. **Origen**

"But we have this treasure in earthen vessels, that the excellency of the power may be of God and not of us." (2 Cor. 4:7) We understand the term "earthen vessels" to refer to the humble diction of the Scriptures. The Greeks

are readily led to despise this humble diction, but in it the
excellency of God's power appears so clearly.

This humble diction did not hinder the mystery of
God's truth and power from traveling to the ends of the
earth. It did not hinder bringing the foolish things of the
world into subjection to the word of Christ, nor some of the
wise as well. For it does not say that *no* wise person
(according to the flesh) is called, only that *not many* who
are wise according to the flesh. **Origen**

If anyone studies them [Paul's writings] attentively, I
am well assured that he will be amazed at the understanding of this man, who can clothe great ideas in
common language. **Origen**

We maintain that it is the object of ambassadors of
truth to present their truths to the greatest number of
people possible. In that way, through their love of men,
they can win over to the side of truth all men without
distinction. That is, the intelligent and the simple, both
Greeks and barbarians. Accordingly, such ambassadors
must use a style of speech that is fitted to do good to all,
and to win over men of every type.

In contrast, the Greeks look down upon the ignorant
as being mere slaves, as being unable to understand a
polished and logical discourse. So they devote their
attention solely to those who have been educated in
literary pursuits.

However, our prophets, and Jesus himself, along with
his apostles, were careful to adopt a manner of speech that
would not only convey the truth but that would be suited
to reach the vast multitudes. For, if I may venture to say,
few people have benefited (if they have been benefited at

all) by the beautiful and polished style of Plato and those who have written like him. Anyone can easily observe that only literary men possess copies of Plato. Now I make these remarks not to disparage Plato (for the world has found him useful), but to point out the aim of those who said, "My speech and my preaching was not with enticing words of man's wisdom, but in demonstration of the Spirit and of power, that our faith should not stand in the wisdom of men, but in the power of God." (1 Cor. 2:4,5) For the Word of God declares that preaching alone is insufficient to reach the human heart, unless God imparts his power to the speaker and bestows his grace upon the speaker's words. This is true even though the preaching in itself is true and most worthy of belief.

We may concede that on certain points a person can find some of the same teachings among the Greeks as in our own Scriptures. Yet, the philosophers do not possess the same power of attracting the souls of men. Nor are they able to empower men to follow such teachings. **Origen**

The Harmony Of The Old And New Testaments

"For whatsoever things were written aforetime were written for our learning." Rom. 15:4

Those who are not skilled in hearing the harmony of God in the sacred Scriptures think that the Old is not in harmony with the New. Or, that the Prophets are not in harmony with the Law. Or, that the Gospels are not in harmony with one another. Or, that the Apostle [Paul] is not in harmony with the Gospel, or with himself, or with the other apostles.

But he who has been instructed in the music of God, being a man wise in word and deed — like David — will bring out the sound of the music of God. For he has learned the right time to strike the chords. First the chords of the Law. Then the Gospel chords in harmony with them. Next, the Prophetic chords. And when reason demands it, the apostolic chords that are in harmony with the Prophetic. And likewise the apostolic chords with those of the Gospels. For such a man knows that all Scripture is the one perfect and harmonized instrument of God. From different sounds, it gives forth one saving voice to those willing to learn. **Origen**

We cannot say of the Holy Spirit's writings that there is anything useless or unnecessary in them, however much they appear obscure to some. What we ought rather to do is to turn the eyes of our mind toward Him who ordered this to be written and to ask of Him their meaning.... Who would dare to say that what is written "by the Word of God" is of no use and makes no contribution to salvation, but is merely a narrative of what happened and was over and done a long time ago, but pertains in no way to us when it is told? **Origen**[1]

Principles Of Bible Interpretation

"Be diligent to present yourself approved to God as a workman who does not need to be ashamed, handling accurately the word of truth." 2 Tim. 2:15 NAS

Since some passages of Scripture are more obscure than others, it is only right that *uncertain* statements should be interpreted by those that are *certain*. Obscure statements should be interpreted by those that are clear and plain. **Tertullian**

The heretics would have the entire revelation of both Testaments yield to merely three passages. However, the only proper course is to understand the *few* statements in the light of the *many* passages. Nevertheless, in their methodology, they are only acting on the principle used by all heretics. **Tertullian**

[1]Origen, *Origen*, trans. and ed. Rowan A. Greer (New York: Paulist Press, 1979), pp. 247, 248. Copyright © 1979 by The Missionary Society of St. Paul the Apostle in the State of New York. Used by permission.

18

Questions Believers Ask

Does God's Foreknowledge Mean That God Causes All Events?

You should not imagine that an event that is predicted through foreknowledge comes to pass *because* it was predicted. Rather, we maintain that he who foretold it was not the *cause* of its happening simply because he foretold it would happen. The future event would have taken place whether or not it had been foretold. It was the future event that afforded the one endowed with foreknowledge to speak of its occurrence in advance.

For example, if you carefully observe the contents of the Psalm, you will find that Judas was considered to be *his own cause* of wickedness. For the psalmist says, "He remembered not to show mercy, but he persecuted the poor and needy man." (Ps. 109:16) **Origen**

Did God Create Evil?

God, who created the world, did not — nor does not — make evil. He only makes what is glorious and excellent. For he who makes it is good. Now man, who was brought into existence, is a creature endowed with the capacity of self-determination. Yet, from this capacity of self-determination, man brings forth what is evil. **Origen**

Come now and let us use the following illustration from the Gospel. There is a certain rock with a little surface soil. If seeds fall upon this layer of soil, they quickly spring up. But after they spring up, they are burned and withered when the sun rises, for they have no root. Now this rock is a human soul, hardened on account of its negligence. It has been changed to stone because of its wickedness. For no one receives a heart created of stone from God. Rather, his heart becomes such because of his own wickedness. **Origen**

For a good reason, God has given man a law for his guidance. It is because man has free will. If man did not possess the power to will and not to will, why would a law have been given? After all, a law is not laid down for an animal devoid of reason. For such an animal, there is only a bridle and a whip. **Hippolytus**

How Can Christians "Test The Spirits"?

*"Beloved, do not believe every spirit, but test the spirits
to see whether they are from God." 1 John 4:1 NAS*

In answer to the subject question, Origen contrasted the
behavior of the oracle of Delphi, also known as the Pythian
priestess, with the conduct of someone truly under the influence
of God's Spirit.

It is not the part of a divine spirit to drive the prophet-
ess into such a state of ecstasy and madness that she loses
control of herself. For he who is under the influence of the
Divine Spirit should be the first to receive the beneficial
effects of that Spirit. Moreover, when a person is in close
communion with God, that should be the time of his
clearest perception.

If then, the Pythian priestess loses control of herself
when she prophesies, what spirit must it be that fills her
mind and clouds her judgment with darkness? Surely
none other than the same type of demons that many
Christians cast out of persons! **Origen**

Why was Abel's Sacrifice Accepted, But Not Cain's?

*"So it came about in the course of time that Cain brought an
offering to the Lord of the fruit of the ground. And Abel, on his
part also brought of the firstborn of his flock and of their fat
portions. And the Lord had regard for Abel and for his offering;
but for Cain and for his offering He had no regard."
Gen. 4:3-5 NAS*

When Abel and Cain offered sacrifices, God did not
look at their gifts, but at their hearts. So the gift was

acceptable if the heart was acceptable. Abel, being peaceable and righteous, sacrificed in innocence to God. He thereby taught others that when they bring their gift to the altar, they should come with the fear of God, with a simple heart, with the law of righteousness, and with the peace of harmony. **Cyprian**

Did Samuel Really Return From The Grave?

"Then the woman said, 'Whom shall I bring up for you?' And he [Saul] said, 'Bring up Samuel for me.' When the woman saw Samuel, she cried out with a loud voice; and the woman spoke to Saul, saying, 'Why have you deceived me? For you are Saul.' And the king said to her, 'Do not be afraid; but what do you see?' And the woman said to Saul, 'I see a divine being coming up out of the earth.' And he said to her, 'What is his form?' And she said, 'An old man is coming up, and he is wrapped with a robe.' And Saul knew that it was Samuel, and he bowed with his face to the ground and did homage. Then Samuel said to Saul, 'Why have you disturbed me by bringing me up?'"
1 Sam. 28:11-15 NAS

The question is often asked whether Samuel really rose from the grave by the hand of the sorceress. Now, if we were to conclude that he really did rise, we would be saying something that is false. For how could a demon call back the soul of anybody — let alone that of a righteous man? Instead, the demon knew what Samuel looked like, so it would have been no difficult matter for the demon to conjure up the form of Samuel.

If that is the case, how did the demon foretell the end of the battle and how Saul would be killed? The demon could easily draw this inference from the wrath of God

against Saul. A physician has no exact knowledge of future
events; yet, seeing a patient past all hope, he can foretell
his death. However, he often errs as to the exact hour of
death. So, too, the demon knew of God's wrath by seeing
Saul's deeds, and by seeing Saul's very attempt to consult
this sorceress. From these things, the demon was able to
foretell Saul's defeat and his death. However, the demon
was in error as to the day of Saul's death. **Hippolytus**

The Meaning Of God "Will Be All In All"

*"Then shall the Son also himself be subject unto him that put
all things under him, that God may be all in all."
1 Cor. 15:28*

I am of the opinion that the expression, "God will be
all in all," (1 Cor. 15:28) means that he will become "all"
in each individual person. How will he become "all" in each
person? It will be when all that any rational understanding can either feel, understand, or think will be
wholly God. It will be when a person's thoughts are
cleansed from the dregs of every sort of evil. It will be when
every cloud of wickedness is completely swept away. It will
be when a person's mind will no longer behold or retain
anything else but God. It is when God will be the measure
and standard of all its movements.

Thus God will be "all," for there will no longer be any
distinction between good and evil, since evil will nowhere
exist. For God is all things, and no evil comes near to him.
To him for whom God is all, there will no longer be any
desire to eat from the tree of the knowledge of good and
evil. And when death shall no longer exist anywhere, nor

even the sting of death, nor any evil at all, then truly God will be "all in all." **Origen**

What Is The Meaning Of "Corban"?

"Moses said, 'Honor your father and your mother'; and, 'He who speaks evil of father or mother, let him be put to death'; but you say, 'If a man says to his father or his mother, anything of mine you might have been helped by is Corban (that is to say, given to God), you no longer permit him to do anything for his father or his mother.'" Mark 7:10-12 NAS

Those who had lent money sometimes said to their debtors (using their language), "That which you owe to me is Corban" — that is, a gift. "For I have dedicated it to the poor, to the account of piety towards God." The debtor was then no longer in debt to the lender, but to God and to piety towards God. The debtor was then obligated, perhaps against his will, to pay the debt to the poor in the name of the lender, to the account of God.

However, what lenders did to debtors was sometimes imitated by sons to their parents. The sons would say, "That which I would otherwise give you, father or mother, you will receive from Corban." The parents, then, upon hearing that which should have been given to them was Corban — consecrated to God — no longer wished to take it from their sons, even though they were in extreme need.

So the Savior condemned this tradition. However, the Pharisees, being lovers of money, approved of this practice. For, under the pretext of being "the poor," they wished to receive that which would have been given to the parents. **Origen**

19

Objections Raised By Unbelievers

How Is Christianity Any Better Than Other Religions?

Celsus, a pagan critic of Christians, raised the following objections to Christianity, which were answered by Origen:

Celsus: Just as you Christians believe in eternal punishments, so do our priests. The same punishment with which you threaten others, they threaten you. Now which of the two religions is more firmly established and true?

Origen: I say that the truth lies with those who are able to move their hearers to live as though what they have heard is true. Christians are moved by the doctrines they hold of the world to come, the rewards of the righteous, and the punishments of the wicked, and they live accordingly. But let Celsus, or anyone else, show us any of *their* people who have been moved in a similar manner by the teaching of pagan priests!

What Evidence Is There That Jesus Was Really Resurrected?

Celsus: The disciples did not really see Jesus after his supposed resurrection from the dead, and they did not really believe in his divinity.

Origen: If this were the case, why were the disciples willing to endure the same sufferings as their Master? Why were they not afraid to incur danger? Why were they willing to leave their native country in order to spread the teachings of Jesus, in accordance with His commandment? If anyone honestly examines the facts, he would have to admit that the disciples would not have devoted themselves to a life of danger for the sake of Jesus' teachings if they had not profoundly believed that what he had taught them was true.

Isn't It Better To Get *All* Of The Facts Before Believing?

If it were possible for everyone to leave the business of life, and devote themselves to the study of wisdom, that would certainly be the best course for all to pursue. But on account of the necessities of life and the weakness of men, such a course is not possible for most persons. Only a few individuals are able to devote themselves earnestly to study. So what better method could be devised for reaching the multitudes than the method that Jesus delivered to the pagans?

Accordingly, the great multitude of believers have washed away the mire of wickedness in which they formerly wallowed. Now let me ask you: Isn't it better that they have become reformed and improved in their habits? Isn't it better that they have believed that men are chastised for sins and honored for good works? Or would it have been better for them not to have become converted on the strength of bare faith? Would it have been better for them to have waited until they could thoroughly examine all of the necessary reasons? If the latter course were followed, few persons would attain this way of life. For most have attained it through a simple faith.

Furthermore, all human activities are dependent upon some type of faith. So isn't it more reasonable to believe in God than to believe in other things? For whoever embarks on a voyage, or enters into a marriage, or becomes the father of children, or plants seed into the ground has faith that better things will result from his actions. He believes this even though the contrary might happen and sometimes does happen. Yet faith that better things will follow makes all men venture upon uncertain enterprises. So why shouldn't our faith in the existence of a God who was the Creator of all these things be reasonably accepted by a person who by faith sails the sea, tills the ground, or marries a wife? **Origen**

Even Unbelievers Call Upon God

When you Romans are tossed about on the sea, with the wind howling furiously, you invoke this one God. If anyone is threatened by any violence, he implores the aid of the one God. If anyone is reduced to the last extremity of poverty and is forced to beg for food, he appeals to God alone.

Thus, you never remember God except when you are in trouble. When fear leaves you, and the dangers have passed, then you quickly hasten back to the temples of the gods. **Lactantius**

The Folly Of Pagan Religions

Pagans sacrifice healthy and fat animals to God, as though he were hungry. They pour forth wine to him, as though he were thirsty. They kindle lights to him, as though he were in darkness.

Does such a man really have full possession of his senses, who presents the light of candles and torches as an offering to him who is the Author and Giver of light? For the light that he requires from us is of a different kind. I am speaking of the light of the mind, which light no one can exhibit unless he has come to know God.

There is no need of animal flesh to appease the majesty of heaven. Rather, what is needed is a pure mind and a just spirit. What is needed is a breast that is generous with a natural love of honorable things. This is true worship: when the mind of the worshipper presents itself as an undefiled offering to God. **Lactantius**

Now, isn't it admittedly the greatest impiety — or rather, the greatest insult, to place the honor of the Divinity at the will and pleasure of human judgment, so that there cannot be a god unless the senate permits him? **Tertullian**

The majesty of your gods are converted into an article of commerce. Men make a business out of their religion. The sanctity of the gods is beggared with sales and contracts. You find a way to even merchandise the grounds of your temples, or the entrance to your altars, or your sacrifices. You make a business out of everything pertaining to your gods. You won't allow them to be worshipped for free. **Tertullian**

It would be far better if I believed in no god at all than to believe in one who is open to doubt or who is full of shame. **Tertullian**

20

Recognizing The Creator

"Lift up your eyes on high,
and behold who hath created these things."
Isa. 40:26

Does it never occur to you to think about and examine whose domain you live in? Whose property you are on? Who owns the earth that you plow? Who owns the air you breathe? Whose water you abundantly enjoy? **Arnobius**

What greater injury could befall a man than for him, surrounded by the order of the universe, to be unable to see the One who made it? What worse affliction could come to anyone other than blindness of the mind, which prevents him from seeing the Creator and Father of every soul? **Origen**

Since God is all-powerful, it is more rational to believe that matter *was* created by him than to believe that the world was *not* made by God. For nothing can be made without mind, intelligence, and design. **Lactantius**

Man: A Marvelous Creation

"And the Lord God formed man of the dust of the ground,
and breathed into his nostrils the breath of life;
and man became a living soul." Gen. 2:7

Man is not merely a rational animal, capable of possessing understanding and knowledge, as the croaking philosophers say. For, according to them, even irrational creatures appear possessed of understanding and knowledge. But man alone is the image and likeness of God. **Tatian**

In the creation of man, a great work was in progress. As often as it experienced the hands of God, the human body received honor. There was honor when human flesh was touched by those hands, and when it was pulled, drawn out, and molded into shape. In your mind, picture God as he was totally employed and absorbed in the creation of man — in His hand, His eye, His work, His purpose, His wisdom, His care, and above all else, in His love. For in the form and expression that God gave to the clay, he had Christ in his thoughts — that one day Christ too would become man. **Tertullian**

Evolution: A Primitive Belief

"The fool hath said in his heart, There is no God." Ps. 14:1

Many people think that the belief that the universe came together by accident is a modern scientific theory. However, the truth of the matter is that this theory was a product of the unscientific age of the ancient world, and it was widely taught during the days of the apostles and early Christians.

When a house or a city is built, it doesn't lay its own stones. The stones do not spontaneously place themselves upon the foundation. Other stones do not lift themselves up to the various layers. Rather, the builder carefully places the skillfully prepared stones in their proper places. In contrast, if the building eventually collapses, the stones are all separated, cast down, and scattered about.

Likewise, when a ship is built, the keel does not lay itself. Nor does the mast erect itself in the center. Rather, the carpenter assembles the materials together in the right way and at the right time. In contrast, if the ship is wrecked at sea, the timbers are broken up and scattered everywhere.

So who can bear to hear it said that this mighty habitation called the universe, composed of the heaven and earth, has been established in all of its order and beauty by those inanimate atoms that are devoid of beauty and order? Who can bear to hear that this state of disorder has grown into this universe, which is true Order itself?

How remarkably civilized these atoms must be! Friends greet and embrace their other atom friends. All are eager to journey together in one habitation. Others, through their own idea, have rounded themselves off into that mighty luminary, the sun, so as to give us daylight. Others have formed themselves into many pyramids of blazing stars so as to crown the whole heavens. All this they do, no doubt, so that the more ordinary atoms might select settlements for themselves!

And from where does this mighty army of fellow-travelers (i.e. atoms) come? They are not marshalled by any captain. None of them are gifted with any comprehension of will. None of them are endowed with any knowledge of each other. Yet, somehow they all hold their course

together in perfect harmony! For the universe is one vast
circular choir that moves in a circular march, moving ever
equally and harmoniously, as it whirls in its orbit.

So who made this universe with its marvelous beauty?
Was it really the irrational army of atoms? Of course not!
Atoms, with their conjunctions, cannot even mold an
image of clay. They cannot even hew and polish a statue
of stone. And if these mere representations and models
cannot be made without the aid of wisdom, how can the
genuine and original patterns of these copies have come
into existence spontaneously? **Dionysius**

The matter from which the universe has been made is
remarkable indeed. I cannot understand how so many
distinguished men hold to the opinion that this matter was
uncreated. That it was not formed by God himself, who is
the Creator of all things. But that its nature and power
were the result of chance. **Origen**

Evidence For A Creator

"The heavens declare the glory of God."
Ps. 19:1

So it seems to me that those people who say that the
whole universe was heaped together by certain atoms
casually adhering to each other — denying that it was
formed by the divine Logos — have neither mind nor
sense. Apparently, they don't even have the ability to *see*.
For what can be more obvious when you lift your eyes up
to the sky, and look around at the things here on earth,

than that there is some Deity of supreme intelligence who governs and nourishes the universe, infusing it with life?

Take the heavens, for example. Notice how far they reach and how rapidly the heavenly bodies move around. See how the sky is adorned by the stars at night and how the sun illuminates it during the day. Surely the marvelous and divine balance of the Supreme Governor is at work here. (Ps. 136:1-9) Look also at the year, how it is made by the circuit of the sun. And look at the month, how the moon formulates it with its phases of increase and decrease. Or how about the recurring pattern of day and night, which provides man with a time for work and a time for rest?

Look also at the sea. It is bound by the law of its shore. And notice the ocean, with its regular ebb and flow of tides. (Job 38:4-11) Look also at the trees, how they are sustained from the depths of the earth. And the fountains, how they gush in perpetual streams. Gaze at the rivers. See how they flow on their same course, year after year. And I haven't even mentioned the ordered peaks of the mountains, the slopes of the hills, and the expanses of the plains.

I could point to the different types of protection provided for the animals. Some are armed with horns; others with teeth. Some have claws; others are barbed with stingers. Some escape danger by the swiftness of their feet, others by soaring into the sky with their wings.

Finally, the very beauty of our own bodies confesses that God is their Designer: Our upright stature and countenance. (Ps. 139:14) The placement of our eyes at the top of our bodies, like a lookout. And the arrangement of the rest of our senses like a citadel. Every member of the body has been designed for the sake of both necessity and beauty. What's even more wonderful is that even though we all have essentially the same bodies, we don't all look alike.

Now, if upon entering a house you found everything well arranged and adorned, you would surely believe that

a master governed the house. You would also recognize
that the master was greater than all of the things in the
house. Therefore, when you look upon the house of the
universe — the heavens and the earth, its laws, and its
order — believe that there is a Lord and Parent of the
universe far more glorious than the stars themselves and
the other parts of the universe. **Mark Felix**

Our Understanding Of Creation Is Not Complete

> *"When I gave my mind to the study of wisdom,*
> *to study all the busy life of the world,*
> *I found that man is unable to grasp*
> *the truth of all that God is doing*
> *in this world."*
> *Eccl. 8:16,17 Moffatt*

Should we think that these things were not made by
God simply because it cannot be plainly explained *how*
they were created? If you had been brought up in a well-
built and lavishly decorated house, would you suppose
that the house was not built by man simply because you
had never seen a workshop? Would you conclude that the
house had not been built by man simply because you did
not know *how* it was built?

Man, in whom nothing is perfect, is nevertheless able
to accomplish more through the use of skill than his feeble
strength alone would permit. This being the case, why
should it appear incredible to you that the world was made
by God? Since he is perfect, wisdom can have no limit, and
strength can have no measure. **Lactantius**

When the saints shall have reached the heavenly abodes, they will clearly see the nature of the stars one by one. And they will comprehend also the other reasons for the works of God. For he himself will reveal it to them. He will show to them, as to children, the causes of things and the power of his creation. He will explain why each star was placed in its particular quarter of the sky. And why it was separated from another star by so great a distance. He will explain what would have been the consequence if that star had been nearer or more remote from others. Or if that star had been larger than another one. He will explain how the totality of things would not have remained the same, but how all things would have been transformed into a different state.

And then when the saints have finished all those matters which are connected with the stars, and with the heavenly orbits, they will come to those things which are not seen. Or to those things whose names we have only heard about. To things that are invisible, which the Apostle Paul has informed us are numerous — although what they are, or what difference may exist among them, we cannot even conjecture by our feeble intellect. And thus our rational nature will grow by each individual step. It will not grow merely as it grew in this life in flesh, body, and soul. Rather, it will be enlarged in understanding and in power of perception. For it will be raised as a mind already perfect to perfect knowledge. It will no longer be impeded at all by our physical senses, but will be increased in intellectual growth. **Origen**

God Is Seen Through His Works

*"For the invisible things of him from the creation
of the world are clearly seen, being understood
by the things that are made." Rom. 1:20*

God cannot be seen by human eyes, but he is seen and
recognized through his providence and his works. If
anyone sees a ship on the sea fully rigged and in sail,
heading for the harbor, he will no doubt infer that there is
a pilot steering the ship. Similarly, we must recognize that
God is the Pilot of the whole universe, even though he is
not visible to human eyes. For he is incomprehensible. A
man cannot even look upon the sun on account of its great
heat and power. Yet, it is a very small heavenly body.
Accordingly, how much more shall a mortal man be unable
to face the glory of God, which is beyond words?
Theophilus

We perceive God from his power, operations, and
creation, although we cannot see him with our eyes. The
voice, the wind, and the sense of smell are examples of
things that we cannot see with our eyes. What is clearer
than the voice? What is stronger than the wind? What are
more compelling than odors? Yet none of those things can
be seen with the eye. Instead, they are perceived by other
parts of the body. In like manner, God is not to be perceived
by us through our eyes or other feeble sensory organs.
Rather, he is beheld by the eyes of the mind, for we can
see his illustrious and wonderful works. **Lactantius**

21

The Blood Of The Martyrs

"Marvel not, my brethren, if the world hate you." 1 John 3:13

We are called "enemies of the people." **Tertullian**

They do not persecute us from the supposition that we are wrong-doers. Rather, they imagine that we are sinning against life itself by the very fact of our being Christians and conducting ourselves accordingly. **Clement**

On the subject of martyrdom the Lord has spoken explicitly, "But I say unto you, whoever shall confess me before men, the Son of man shall also confess before the angels of God. But whoever shall deny me before men, I will deny before the angels." **Clement**

The command has been given me not to make mention of any other god, not to worship any other god, and not to

in any way show reverence to another other than the One
who so commands me. Him I fear, that I may not be
forsaken by him. Him I love with my whole being, that I
may die for him. Serving as a soldier of God under this
oath of allegiance, I am challenged by the enemy. If I
surrender to them, I become one of them. So to maintain
this oath, I fight furiously in battle. I am wounded; I am
hacked to pieces and slain. He who endures to the end, let
that man be saved. (Matt. 24:13) **Tertullian**

We have learned from the Gospel neither to relax our
efforts in times of peace, giving ourselves up to leisure, nor,
when the world makes war upon us, to become cowards
and apostatize from the love of the God of all things.
Origen

Who is so arrogant — who is so puffed up — so as to
forbid me to raise my eyes to heaven? Who can impose
upon me the necessity either of worshipping that which I
am unwilling to worship, or of abstaining from worshipping the One I do wish to worship? So long as we have any
courage to despise death and pain, no one can do this!
Lactantius

How foolish that the world calls us criminals because
we are willing to die for God. Yet, those who are willing to
die for a *man* are extolled to the heavens with the highest
of praises. **Lactantius**

The Two Kinds Of Persecution

"There is no one who has left house or brothers or sisters or mother or father or children or farms, for My sake and for the gospel's sake, but that he shall receive a hundred times as much now in the present age, houses, and brothers and sisters and mothers and children and farms, along with persecutions."
Mark 10:30 NAS

Then what about the expression, "with persecutions"? By this, he means that we must not grasp at money, property and family. You see, there are two kinds of persecutions. One kind comes from the outside. It comes from men who attack God's faithful people, because of hatred, envy, greed, or demonic pressure. But the most painful kind of persecution is that which is *internal*. This persecution comes from each person's own soul, as the soul is plagued by irreverent lusts, diverse pleasures, earthly hopes, and destructive dreams. It is always grasping for more. Maddened by savage loves, it is inflamed by the passions that attack it like stinging insects. In the end, it leads a person to give up hope for [eternal] life, and to have contempt for God.

Internal persecution is more painful because it is always with a person. The persecuted one cannot escape it, because he carries the enemy everywhere inside himself. The persecution that comes from outside is merely a trial. But what comes from inside produces death. The war from without may be easily ended, but the internal war in our souls continues until the day we die.

So, in light of this persecution, abandon whatever leads you to evil — whether it be your worldly wealth or your fleshly brothers and other pledges. Instead, procure peace for yourself by freeing yourself from these prolonged persecutions. Turn from them to the Gospel. Above everything else, choose the Savior and Advocate and

Paraclete of your soul, the Prince of life. "For the things
that are seen are temporary; but the things that are not
seen are eternal." (2 Cor. 4:18) In the present life,
everything is vanishing and insecure. But what is to come
is eternal life. **Clement**

We Should Not Seek Out Martyrdom

If he who kills a man of God sins against God, then he
who causes a Christian to be brought before the tribunal
is also guilty of that Christian's death. And so is the
Christian who does not avoid persecution, but rather
voluntarily presents himself to be captured. As a result,
such a Christian becomes an accomplice in the crime of his
persecutor.

Unbelievers ask us why God does not help us when we
are persecuted. But, as far as we are concerned, what
wrong is being done to us in being released by death to go
to the Lord? We simply undergo a change of life.
Clement

Faithfulness is a virtue. Yet, we do not resist those who
injure us, for we must yield to them. (Matt. 5:39) Yet, when
men command us to disobey the law of God and to oppose
what is right, we must choose the command of God over
the command of men. And no threats or punishments
should deter us.

For it is a virtue to scorn death. Not that we *seek* death,
nor do we inflict it upon ourselves. That is what many of
the distinguished philosophers did, but that is a wicked
and ungodly thing. Nevertheless, when we are commanded to desert God and to betray our faith, we should prefer

to suffer death. Thus with lofty and invincible minds we trample upon those things that others fear — pain and death. This is virtue: to stand resolute in this one thing alone — that no terror and no violence can turn us away from God. **Lactantius**

How Persecution Benefits The Church

"My circumstances have turned out for the greater progress of the gospel, so that my imprisonment in the cause of Christ has become well known." Phil. 1:12,13

Persecution is the fan which cleanses the Lord's threshing floor — that is, the church. It winnows the mixed heap of believers, separating the wheat of the martyrs from the chaff of the deniers. **Tertullian**

All of the devices of men against Christians have been brought to nothing. For the more that kings, rulers, and peoples have persecuted us, the more we have increased in number and grown in strength. **Origen**

One reason why God permits persecution is so that the number of his people may be increased. And it is not difficult to show why persecution has this effect. First, great numbers of people are driven from the worship of the false gods by their hatred of the cruelty inflicted on us. Secondly, some are attracted by virtue and faith itself. Some begin to suspect that it is not without reason that the worship of the gods is considered evil by so many people. They realize there must be a reason why persons would rather die than to do what others do in order to preserve their lives.

People want to know what good thing it is that is defended even to death. What is it that is preferred to all things that are pleasant and beloved in this life? What is it that neither the loss of property, nor imprisonment in a dark prison, nor bodily pain or tortures can deter Christians from? These things have a profound impact on others. **Lactantius**

The more often we are slain by you, the more in number we grow. The blood of Christians is seed. For who that contemplates it is not eager to inquire what is at the bottom of it? And who after making inquiry does not end up embracing our teachings? **Tertullian**

Christians Should Not Persecute Others

Around A.D. 275, Archelaus, an orthodox Christian bishop, entered into a public debate with Manes, an heretical teacher who belonged to the Manichean sect. The debate had been arranged by Marcellus, a wealthy Christian known for his works of charity. Archelaus soundly defeated Manes in the debate, and the following is an account of what occurred afterwards:

On hearing these matters, those who were present gave great glory to God, and justly praised Him. They also bestowed tokens of honor on Archelaus. Then Marcellus arose. Casting aside his cloak, he threw his arms around Archelaus and kissed him. He embraced him and clung to him. However, the children who had chanced to gather around the place of debate began pelting Manes with rocks in order to drive him off. The rest of the crowd began to follow their example and rose up excitedly with the intention of chasing Manes away with stones.

But when Archelaus observed this, he raised his voice like a trumpet above the din, being anxious to restrain the crowd. He addressed them, "Stop, my beloved brethren! Otherwise, we may be found to have bloodguilt on us at the Day of Judgment. For it was written of men like Manes, 'There must be heresies among you that those who are approved may be made manifest among you.'"(1 Cor. 11:19) And after he had spoken these words, the crowds of people were quieted again. **Archelaus**

The Safety Of The Church
Is In God's Hands

"Upon this rock I will build My church;
and the gates of Hades shall not overpower it."
Matt. 16:18 NAS

When God gives the Tempter permission to persecute us, we suffer persecution. And when God wishes us to be free from suffering, even though surrounded by a world that hates us, we enjoy a wonderful peace. We trust in the protection of the One who said, "Be of good cheer, for I have overcome the world." And truly he *has* overcome the world. From his victory, we take courage. Even again if he should wish for us to suffer and contend for our faith, let the enemy come against us. We will say to them, "I can do all things through Christ Jesus our Lord who strengthens me." **Origen**

But with regard to the Christians, they are taught not to avenge themselves upon their enemies. They observe laws of a mild and loving character. And because they would not have made war, even if they had been given authority to do so, they have obtained this reward from God: that he has always fought on their behalf.

On certain occasions, he has restrained those who rose up against Christians and desired to destroy them. However, some individual Christians, who can be easily numbered, have endured death for the sake of Christianity. God allowed this for the purpose of strengthening the rest: that by seeing a few contending for their faith, the others would be put on guard and would be better prepared to scorn death. But God has not permitted the whole Church to be exterminated. Rather, he has desired that it should continue and that the whole world should be filled with this beneficial and religious doctrine.
Origen

We do not seek for anyone to be unwillingly compelled to worship our God, who is the God of all men. Nor are we angry if anyone does not worship him. For we trust in his majesty and power to avenge any contempt shown towards him. Likewise, he has the power to avenge the persecution and wrongs inflicted on his servants. Therefore, when we suffer such unrighteous things, we do not resist — even in word. Rather, we leave vengeance to God.   **Lactantius**

22

World Conquerors

*"And they overcame him because of the blood of the Lamb
and because of the word of their testimony, and
they did not love their life even to death."*
Rev. 12:11 NAS

The following passages were all written by men who gained victory over the world, willingly suffering death because of their love for God.

You strive earnestly to make us deny the name of Christ. Yet, we choose death instead. For we have the full assurance that God will reward us with all the good that he has promised. Still, in addition to all this, we pray for you, that Christ may have mercy upon you. **Justin Martyr**

When you hear that we seek a kingdom, you suppose — without making any inquiry — that we speak of a human kingdom. But that is not so. We are speaking of a kingdom that is with God. (John 18:36) That is why we so openly confess our faith when charged with being Christians, even though we know that death is the punishment for our confession. If we were looking for a human kingdom, we would simply deny our Christ in order to escape death. We would do our utmost to conceal the fact that we are Christians, so that we might live to attain such a human kingdom. But since our thoughts are not fixed on the present, we are not concerned when men kill us. We recognize that death is a debt that we must eventually pay anyway. **Justin Martyr**

It is necessary, therefore, to not only be *called* by the name "Christian," but to actually *be* a Christian. If we are not ready to die in the same manner of His suffering, His life is not in us. **Ignatius**

Bring on the fire and the cross. Bring on the packs of wild beasts. Let there be the breaking and dislocating of my bones and the severing of my limbs. Bring on the mutilation of my whole body. In fact, bring on all the diabolical tortures of Satan. Only let me attain to Jesus Christ! I would rather die for Jesus Christ than to reign over the ends of the entire earth. **Ignatius**

Do Not Fear Man

> *"Have no fear of those who kill the body but
> cannot kill the soul: rather fear Him who can
> destroy both soul and body in Gehenna."*
> *Matt.10:28 Moffatt*

Do you fear man, O Christian? You who ought to be feared by the angels since you are to judge angels? You who ought to be feared by evil spirits, since you have received power also over evil spirits? You who ought to be feared by the whole world, since by you the world, too, is judged? When you flee from the devil in fear, you give yourself back to him, and you treat Christ, who is in you, as of small account. **Tertullian**

The one who knows God will most gladly depart from this life out of his love for the Lord. Perhaps he will even thank the one who executed him and the one who laid the plot against him. He will thank them for providing him with an opportunity to show his love for the Lord by his patient suffering. With good courage, then, he goes to the Lord, his friend, for whom he voluntarily gave his body and his soul. Because he follows the Savior in life and death, he hears from the Savior the words of poetry — "Dear brother." We call martyrdom "perfection," not because the martyr has now completed his life, but because he has demonstrated the perfect work of love.

Now some of the heretics have not understood the Lord. They have an unholy and cowardly love of life. They say that the true martyrdom* is to have knowledge of the only true God (which we also admit), and that the person who confesses Christ unto death is actually committing suicide and is guilty of murdering himself. And they invent other justifications for cowardice. Now, we, also, teach that those who rush headlong unto death [i.e., seeking martyrdom] are not true martyrs, even though they are publicly executed. **Clement**

---

*The Greek word translated "martyrdom" also means "testimony."

Tertullian's Exhortation To Christians In Prison:

Once you entered the prison gate, you were severed from the rest of the world — including the ordinary course of worldly life and all of its affairs. Do not let this separation from the world alarm you. If you reflect upon it for a moment, you will realize that it is really the world that is the prison. I see that you have gone *out* of a prison, rather than *into* one. The world is darker than the prison, for it blinds not only the eyes, but the hearts of men. The shackles of the world are more severe, for they bind the very souls of men. The odors of the world — human lusts — are worse than those of a prison. In fact, the world contains the larger number of criminals — the whole human race, who are criminals against God.

So think of yourselves as having been transported from a prison to a haven. True, the prison is full of darkness, but you yourselves are light. Unpleasant smells are there, but you are a sweet odor before God. You daily wait in expectation of the judge, but in the end, you will judge the judges themselves. Sadness may be there in prison for him who yearns for the world's enjoyments. But, remember, the Christian outside the prison has renounced the world, too. It doesn't matter *where* you are in the world, for you are not of it.

Meanwhile, let us compare the life of the world and that of the prison to see if the spirit does not gain more in the prison than the flesh loses. Nay, by the care of the church and the love of the brothers, even the flesh does not lose what is for its good while it is in prison. Meanwhile, the spirit obtains some important advantages. While in prison, you have no occasion to have to look upon strange gods. You are not pained by the noise of the public shows, nor by the atrocities, madness, or immodesty that goes on there. Your eyes do not have to see any more brothels. You are free from causes of offense and from temptations. You are also free from persecution.

The prison does the same service for the Christian that the desert did for the prophets. Our Lord himself spent much of his time in seclusion, that he might be free from the world and have greater liberty to pray. In fact, it was in the solitude of a mountain that he showed his glory to the disciples. So let us drop the name of prison and instead call it a place of retirement.

Though the flesh is confined, the spirit is still free. So, in spirit, roam abroad. Walk about in spirit, not following shady paths or long colonnades. Rather, follow the way that leads to God. As often as your footsteps are on this way, in spirit, that often you will not be in bonds. The leg does not feel the chain when the mind is in heaven.

Yet, blessed ones, even if we grant that the prison is unpleasant, remember that we are called to the warfare of the living God. Now, no soldier goes out to battle laden with luxuries. He does not go into action from his comfortable chambers, but from a lightweight and narrow tent. In the military camp, there is every kind of hardness, roughness, and unpleasantness to tolerate.

In like manner, O blessed ones, count whatever is hard in this lot of yours as a discipline of your powers of mind and body. You are about to pass through a noble struggle, in which the living God acts the part of the master of ceremonies. In this struggle, the Holy Spirit is your trainer, and the prize to be won is an eternal crown of angelic essence — citizenship in the heavens, glory everlasting.

Therefore, your Master, Jesus Christ, who has anointed you with his Spirit, has seen it good to take you from a more pleasant condition before the day of conflict. He has imposed on you a harder treatment so that your strength might be the greater when you are led forth to the arena. Even the world's athletes are given a more

stringent regimen so that their physical powers will be
built up. Yet, as the apostle says, "they do it that they may
obtain a corruptible crown." (1 Cor. 9:25) In contrast, we
have an eternal crown in our eye. So look upon the prison
as your training ground.

Let the spirit communicate with the flesh about our
common salvation, thinking no longer of the troubles of
the prison, but of the struggle and conflict for which they
are the preparation. The flesh, perhaps, will dread the
merciless sword, the lofty cross, the rage of the wild beasts,
the punishment of the flames — of all the most terrible —
and the sinister skill of the executioner in torture. On the
other hand, let the spirit set clearly before both itself and
the flesh, how even worldly people have calmly endured
these things, though they were exceedingly painful. In
fact, men and women of the world have eagerly desired
these things merely for the sake of fame and glory.

Now, if so high a value is put on the earthly glory, won
by mental and bodily vigor, that men, for the glory of their
fellowman, have disdained the sword, the fire, the cross,
the wild beasts, and torture, then such things are surely
but trifling sufferings to obtain a celestial glory and a
divine reward. If the bit of glass is so precious, what must
the true pearl be worth? Are we not called on, then, to most
joyfully lay out as much for the true crown as others do for
the false? **Tertullian**

The Victory Of Martyrdom

*"Do not fear what you are about to suffer. Behold, the devil is
about to throw some of you into prison, that you may be tested,
and for ten days you will have tribulation. Be faithful unto
death, and I will give you the crown of life. He who has an ear,
let him hear what the Spirit says to the churches. He who
conquers shall not be hurt by the second death."*
Rev. 2:10,11 RSV

When people see that we are lacerated by various kinds of tortures yet remain unsubdued even when our very torturers are worn out, they come to believe that the agreement of so many people and the unyielding faith of the dying is not without meaning. They realize that human perseverance alone could not endure such tortures without the aid of God. Even robbers and men of robust frame are unable to endure tortures of this kind. But among us, boys and delicate women — not to speak of men — silently overcome their torturers. Even the fire is unable to extort a groan from them. These persons — the young and the weaker sex — do not endure the burning and mutilation of their whole bodies because they have no other choice. They could easily avoid this punishment if they wished to, by denying Christ. But they endure it willingly because they put their trust in God. **Lactantius**

You think we're being punished when we suffer hardships and infirmities. But it's not punishment — it's warfare. Fortitude is strengthened by infirmities. (Jas. 1:12) Virtue and suffering usually go hand in hand. Both the body and the mind grow sluggish without hard work. Think of all the mighty men you hold up as examples. Wasn't it their afflictions that made them great? God is not unable to aid us, as you have claimed, nor does he despise us. He loves his own people, and he is the ruler of all men. However, he tests us and searches us through adversities. He tests the qualities of all of us through trials, often even to death itself. He can test us to the point of death because he knows that nothing can perish to him. Just as gold is refined by the fire, so are we proven through times of crisis. (Mal. 3:3)

It is a beautiful spectacle to God when a Christian battles pain — or when he stands up to threats, punishment, and torture. When he mocks both the horrors of the executioner and the roar of the crowd screaming for his death. When he stands up to kings and princes as a free man, yielding only to God, to whom he belongs. And when he is triumphant and victorious, he tramples on the very man who has pronounced his death sentence. For the one who obtains the prize for which he has contended — he is the conqueror. (Rev. 2:10,11)

What soldier, when under the eyes of his general, would not incur peril with greater boldness? No one receives a reward before his trial. Yet a general can't give what is beyond his power. He can't give life to the soldier. He can only bestow glory and honor for the warfare. In contrast, God's soldier is neither forsaken in his suffering nor is he brought to an end by death. So although you think we Christians must be miserable, we are not at all. (Matt. 5:11,12; 10:28)

You praise to the skies the sufferings of your brave men. Take Mucius Scaevola, for example. When his attempt to kill the invading king failed, he bravely sacrificed his right hand in the fire. And his life was spared because of his heroism. Yet look at how many of our people have not only allowed their right hands to be burned, but their whole bodies as well. And they have endured this without any cries of pain, even though it was in their power to avoid this punishment [by simply renouncing Christ]. And I'm not just comparing our *men* with Mucius Scaevola. For even our boys and young women treat your crosses, tortures, wild beasts, and other horrors with contempt and patient suffering. Don't you realize that *nobody* is willing to endure such punishment without a reason? That nobody is able to endure such tortures without help from God? **Mark Felix**

23

Of Whom The World Was Not Worthy

"They were stoned, they were sawn in two, they were tempted, they were put to death with the sword ... men of whom the world was not worthy."
Heb. 11:37,38 NAS

The following passages are descriptions of the pilgrim walk of the early Christians, as taken from writings of the second and third centuries.

An Anonymous Description

Christians are not distinguished from other men by country, language, or the customs which they observe. They don't inhabit cities of their own, and they do not use any special form of speech. In short, they lead a life that is not marked by any peculiarity. For their course of conduct was not devised through any sort of human speculation. Nor was it produced through the deliberations of thinkers. In fact, unlike some, they do not proclaim that they are following *any* human doctrines.

Rather, as the lot of each of them may have fallen, they
live in both Greek and barbarian cities. Although they
follow the local customs as to food, clothing, and the rest
of their ordinary conduct, yet they display to us their
wonderful and confessedly striking method of life. They
dwell in their own countries simply as sojourners. As
citizens, they share in all things with others, and yet they
endure all things as though they were foreigners. Every
foreign land is just like their native country to them. And
every land of their birth is as a land of strangers.

Like others, they marry and beget children. However,
they do not destroy their offspring. They have a common
table, but not a common bed. Although they live *in* the
flesh, they do not live *after* the flesh. They pass their days
on earth, but they are citizens of heaven. They obey the
laws of the land, but, at the same time, they surpass these
laws by their lives. They love all men; yet, they are
persecuted by all. They are unknown and condemned.
Even though they are put to death, they are restored to
life. They are poor. Yet, they make many rich. They are
needy in all things; yet, they abound in all. Although they
are dishonored, in their very dishonor they are glorified.

Even though people speak evil of them, they are
righteous. They are reviled; yet, they bless. They are
insulted, but they repay insults with honor. Although they
do good, they are punished as criminals. When punished,
they rejoice as though infused with life. The Jews attack
them as foreigners, and the Greeks persecute them. Yet,
those who hate them are unable to give any reason for
their hatred. **Anonymous**

A Description From Mark Felix

As for us, our modesty is not a matter of outward show. Rather, in our hearts we gladly abide by the bonds of a single marriage. In the desire to procreate, we know either one wife or none at all. In our banquets, we share our food with one another. Not only are our banquets modest, they are also sober. For we do not prolong our feasts with wine or indulge in entertainments. Rather, we temper our joy with seriousness, with chaste conversation, and with bodies even more chaste. (Eph. 5:3,4) In fact, many of us remain virgins our entire lives. (Matt. 19:10-12; 1 Cor. 7:26-34) We *enjoy* our virginity rather than boasting about it. We are so far from indulging in incestuous lusts that some of us blush about even modest intermingling of the sexes.

And just because we refuse your honors and purple robes doesn't mean that you should view us as the lowest of people. We are easy to please. We assemble together with the same quietness with which we live our personal lives. (Rom. 12:18) You say that we are talkative only in corners, but the truth is that you are afraid to hear us in public. The fact that our numbers increase day by day is no cause to criticize us; it is instead a praiseworthy testimony. We *keep* our members because we live an unblemished lifestyle, and we *increase* our numbers by the addition of new converts.

Furthermore, we do not recognize our members by some small bodily mark, as you have claimed. Rather, we know one another by the signs of innocence and modesty. To your regret, we love one another with a mutual love, because we do not know how to hate. (John 13:35) To your envy, we call one another brothers, for we are all born of one God — one Parent. We are companions in faith and fellow-heirs in hope.

We carry our wisdom in our minds — not in our robes.
We don't speak great things — we live them.   **Mark Felix**

A Description From Justin Martyr

The teachings of Jesus have transformed our lives. We
who previously delighted in immorality now embrace
chastity exclusively. We who used to practice magical arts
now devote our lives to the good and unbegotten God. We
who valued the acquisition of wealth and possessions
above all things now bring what we have into a common
pool and share with everyone in need. (Acts 4:32) Many of
us used to hate and destroy one another; we would not live
with people of a different race because of their different
customs. But now, since the coming of Christ, we live
closely with such people, and we pray for our enemies. We
seek to persuade those who unjustly hate us to live by the
wonderful teachings of Christ so that they can enjoy the
wonderful hope of God's reward with us.

Christ also taught us to suffer patiently, to be ready to
serve all others, and to be free from anger. 'If a man strikes
you on one cheek, offer the other to him also. And do not
hinder the one who would take away your cloak or coat.
Whoever stays angry is in danger of the fire of punishment. If anyone compels you to go with him a mile, go two.
And let your good works shine before men that, upon
seeing them, they may glorify your Father in heaven.'
(Luke 6:29; Matt. 5:22,41,16)

Christ also taught us not to struggle with others, or to
imitate wicked people. Rather, he urged us to lead all
people away from dishonor and wickedness by our
patience and gentleness. The fact that we actually follow
his teachings is demonstrated by the many Christians who

once followed your way of thinking. Now they have
changed their violent and oppressive dispositions. Some
of them were won to Christianity by the righteousness
they observed in the life of their Christian neighbors.
Others were won by the extraordinary restraint Christian
travelers displayed when they were cheated. Still others
were attracted by the honesty of the Christians with whom
they transacted business. **Justin Martyr**

Children Of Peace

"For though we walk in the flesh,
we do not war after the flesh." 2 Cor. 10:3

"Blessed are the peacemakers:
for they shall be called the children of God." Matt. 5:9

"But I say unto you, Love your enemies, bless them that curse
you, do good to them that hate you, and pray for them which
despitefully use you, and persecute you." Matt. 5:44

We have learned the true worship of God from the law
and the word that went forth from Jerusalem by means of
the apostles of Jesus. And so we have fled for safety to the
God of Jacob and the God of Israel. Throughout the whole
earth, we who were formerly filled with war, mutual
slaughter, and every wickedness, have each changed our
warlike weapons. That is, we have changed our swords
into ploughshares and our spears into instruments of
cultivation. What do we cultivate? Holiness, righteousness, love of man, faith, and hope. We have these things
from the Father himself through the One who was
crucified. And we sit each one under his vine — that is,

each man possesses his own married wife. **Justin Martyr**

We have learned not to return blow for blow. Not only that, we do not take to court those who plunder and rob us. Rather, we offer the other cheek to those who hit us on one side of the face. To those who take away our coat, we also give our inner cloak. But when we have surrendered our property, they plot against our very bodies and lives. **Athenagoras**

When you know that we cannot bear even to see a man put to death, although justly, who of you can accuse us of murder or cannibalism? Who among you does not consider the fights of gladiators and wild beasts to be of the greatest interest? Especially those contests sponsored by the emperor? Yet, since we consider watching a man put to death to be nearly the same as killing him, we shun such spectacles. How then could we put people to death — we who do not even watch people being killed lest we should contract guilt and pollution. And we say that those women who use drugs to bring on abortion are committing murder. We say that they will have to give an account to God for the abortion. So how could we possibly commit murder? It hardly makes sense that the same person who regards the very fetus in the womb as a created being — and therefore an object of God's care — would kill him when he has passed into life. **Athenagoras**

To those who ask us where we have come from, or who is our founder, we reply: "We have come in harmony with the teachings of Jesus. We have beaten our hostile swords into ploughshares. And we have converted into pruning hooks the spears we formerly used in war. For we no longer take up 'sword against nation,' nor do we 'learn war anymore.' For we have become children of peace for the sake of Jesus, who is our leader." **Origen**

A People Without Class Distinctions

"There is neither Jew nor Greek,
there is neither bond nor free,
there is neither male nor female:
for ye are all one in Christ Jesus."
Gal. 3:28

The philosophers do not allow any to enter upon their way of philosophy except boys and young men. For they say that knowledge is learned best at a young age. In contrast, we lead those of each sex, every age, and every race into this heavenly path. For God, who is the Guide of the heavenly way, denies immortality to no human being. **Lactantius**

Among us you will find uneducated persons, craftsmen, and old women. If some are unable in words to prove the benefit of our teachings, their very deeds demonstrate the benefit arising from their firm belief that our teachings are true. Rather than rehearsing speeches, they practice good works. When struck, they do not strike back. When robbed, they do not go to law. They give to those who ask of them. And they love their neighbors as themselves. **Athenagoras**

We treat our ordinary neighbors the same as we would treat emperors. For we are equally forbidden to wish ill, to do ill, speak ill, or to think ill of any person. The thing we must not do to an emperor, we must not do to any one else. Since we are commanded to love our enemies, whom have we to hate? If injured, we are forbidden to retaliate, lest we become as bad ourselves. So who can suffer injury at our hands? **Tertullian**

In God's sight, no one is a slave; no one is a master. Since we all have the same Father, we are all equally his children. No one is poor in God's sight except the one lacking in justice. No one is rich except the one with an abundance of virtues. The reason why neither the Romans nor the Greeks could possess justice was that they had so many class distinctions: The rich and the poor. The powerful and the lowly. The highest authority of kings, and the common individual.

However, someone may say, "Isn't it true that among Christians some are poor and others are rich? Some are masters and others are servants? Isn't there some distinction between persons?" But there is none. In fact, the very reason we call each other brothers is that we believe we are all equal. Although the physical circumstances of Christian lives may differ, we view no persons as servants. Instead, we speak of them — and treat them — as brothers in spirit and as fellow-servants of Christ. **Lactantius**

In contrast, look at the heretics who hold a different view of the grace of Christ than that which has come to us. How opposed they are to the will of God! They have no regard for love. They have no care for the widow, the orphan, or the oppressed. Nor do they care for the bonds-man or the free; the hungry or the thirsty. **Ignatius**

A Chaste People

> *"For this is the will of God, your sanctification; that is, that you abstain from sexual immorality; that each of you know how to possess his own vessel in sanctification and honor, not in lustful passion, like the Gentiles who do not know God." 1 Thess. 4:3-5 NAS*

We are so far from practicing sexual immorality that it is not lawful among us to even enjoy a lustful look. For he said, "He that looks on a woman to lust after her has already committed adultery in his heart." (Matt. 5:28) On this account, too, according to age, we recognize some as sons and daughters. Others we regard as brothers and sisters. To the more advanced in life we give the honor due to fathers and mothers. On behalf of those, then, to whom we apply the names of brothers and sisters, and other designations of family relationship, we exercise the greatest care that their bodies should remain pure and undefiled. **Athenagoras**

24

Children Of The Kingdom

"My kingdom is not of this world." John 18:36

I do not wish to be a king. I am not anxious to be rich.
I decline military command. I detest immorality. I am not
impelled by an insatiable love of gain so as to go to sea. I
do not strive for athletic crowns. I am free from a mad
thirst for fame. I scoff at death. I am above every kind of
disease. Grief does not consume my soul. If I am a slave, I
endure servitude. If I am free, I do not boast of my good
birth. I see that the same sun is for all, and there is one
death for all, whether they live in pleasure or poverty.
Tatian

Ezekiel said, "If anyone is a good man, doing what is
right and honest; if he does not eat meat with the blood in
it; if he does not worship the idols of Israel; if he does not
seduce his neighbor's wife nor touch an unclean woman;
if he oppresses no one but returns what his debtor has
pledged; if he robs no one; if he feeds the hungry and
clothes the naked; if he takes no interest on a loan; if he

168

abstains from crime and decides fairly between man and man; if he lives by my laws; if he observes and obeys my rules; then he is a righteous man. He shall surely live, says the Lord." (Ezek. 18:5-9) These words contain a description of the conduct of Christians. **Clement**

You Romans are in the habit of saying about us, "Lucius Titius is a good man, only he is a Christian." Or, someone else will say, "I wonder that so worthy a man as Caius Seius has become a Christian." For some reason, it occurs to no one that perhaps the reason why a man is good and wise is *because* he is a Christian. Or, the reason why a person became a Christian was because he was wise and good. **Tertullian**

We Christians are nothing else than worshippers of the Supreme King and Head, under our Master, Christ. If you make careful examination, you will find that nothing else is implied in our religion. For that is the sum total of all that we do. This is the proposed end and limit of sacred duties.

Before Him we all prostrate ourselves, according to our custom. We adore Him in common prayers. From Him we ask for those things that are just, honorable, and worthy of his ear. Not that he needs our supplications, or that he loves to see the worship of so many thousands laid at his feet. No, such worship is actually for *our* benefit.

Because of our innate weakness, we are prone to err and to yield to various lusts and desires. For that reason, he allows himself to be comprehended in our thoughts. Thereby, while we entreat him and strive to merit his bounties, we may receive a desire for purity. **Arnobius**

A People Separated From The World

*"They are not of the world,
even as I am not of the world."
John 17:16*

It is well known that Christians are a sort of people who are always ready to die. Therefore, some people imagine that the sole purpose of our training in the type of abstinence [of worldly pleasures] we practice is so it will be easier for us to give up this life. In other words, they think our abstinence already severs our ties to the present life. They regard our abstinence as an art of quenching all desire for life. For as far as they are concerned, we have emptied life of all those things that make life desirable.

So they view our abstinence as merely a matter of human planning and foresight. However, in truth, it is something clearly laid down by divine command. To be sure, it would be a grievous thing for Christians to die for God while enjoying the sumptuous pleasures [of this life]. Nevertheless, it is still not as the pagans say. **Tertullian**

Do we have to ask the pagans themselves about this? Let them tell us whether it is right for Christians to attend the shows. Why, the rejection of these amusements is the primary sign to them that a man has adopted the Christian faith. **Tertullian**

A Disciplined Church

> *"But now I have written unto you not to keep company,*
> *if any man that is called a brother be a fornicator, or*
> *covetous, or an idolater ... Therefore put away*
> *from among yourselves that wicked person."*
> *1 Cor. 5:11,13*

You say that we are a most shameful throng and that we are utterly steeped in luxury, wickedness, and depravity. We will not deny that this is true of some who profess to be Christians. Even the healthiest and purest body usually has a mole, a wart, or freckles on it. Even the sky itself is not ever *perfectly* clear so as not to be flecked with some wispy cloud. However, any persons who conduct themselves in the way you have described do not assemble with us. Neither do they belong to our communion. By their delinquency, they become yours once more. You have no right to call those persons "Christians," to whom we Christians ourselves deny that name. **Tertullian**

In the lax discipline of the heretics, we have a measure of their doctrine. They say that God is *not* to be feared. Therefore, in their opinion, all things are free and unrestrained. In contrast, among us, where there is the fear of God, there is seriousness. There is an honorable and yet careful diligence. Admission into our ministry is made carefully and with a lot of consideration. Our communion is safely guarded. There is a scrupulous submission to authority and a united church. And, yes, there is God in all things. **Tertullian**

True And False Christians

*"Not every one that saith unto me, Lord, Lord, shall enter
into the kingdom of heaven; but he that doeth the will of my
Father which is in heaven." Matt. 7:21*

On this account, those who hear the word powerfully
proclaimed are filled with power. They demonstrate this
both by their dispositions and their lives. They struggle on
behalf of the truth even unto death. On the other hand,
some are altogether empty. Although they profess to
believe in God through Jesus, they do not possess any
divine power. They only have the *appearance* of being
converted to the word of God. **Origen**

For we assert that the whole inhabited world contains
evidence of the works of Jesus in the very existence of
those churches of God that have been founded through
him. In these churches you will find many who have been
converted from the practice of innumerable sins. And the
name of Jesus can still remove impediments from the
minds of men. It can still expel demons and take away
diseases. It can produce a marvelous meekness of spirit
and complete change of character and humanity. It can
produce a goodness and gentleness. That is, it can produce
these things in those who do not *pretend* to be Christians
simply for the sake of subsistence or to have their physical
needs supplied. Rather, these things are produced in those
who have honestly accepted the doctrine concerning God
and Christ, and the judgment to come. **Origen**

What The Pagans Said About Christians

Celsus: Christians should be made to make their choice between two alternatives. If they refuse to render due service to the gods, and to respect those who are set over this service, let them not come to manhood, or marry wives, or have children, or indeed take any share in the affairs of life. But let them depart from this world with all speed, leaving no posterity behind them, so that this race of Christians may become extinct from the face of the earth.

Origen: To this we reply that there appears no good reason to us for leaving this world, except when piety and virtue require it. An example is when those who are set up as judges think that they have power over our lives, and place before us the choice to either live in violation of the commands of Jesus, or else to die if we continue obedient to those commands.

I, along with others who worship the Creator, will live according to the laws of God, never consenting to obey the laws of sin. We will marry if we wish and bring up the children given to us in marriage. We will not only partake of the blessings of life, but we will bear its appointed sorrows as a trial for our souls. For the divine Scriptures speak of human afflictions as being the fire that refines gold. So the spirit of man is refined through trials. Through these trials it is found to be worthy of either condemnation or praise.

We say that the person who truly discharges the responsibilities of life is the one who is ever mindful of who his Creator is. He is the one who remembers what things are agreeable to God, and he acts in all things in a manner that would please God.

Celsus: You Christians should take part in the government of our country, when that is required, to maintain law and order and to support religion.

Origen: We recognize that in every nation there exists another national organization, founded by the Logos of God. We exhort those who are mighty in word and of blameless life to rule over *churches*. But we reject those who are ambitious to rule. Instead, we use those who, because of an abundance of modesty, are not inclined to take an office of oversight in the Church of God. Those who rule well over us are under the restraining influence of the great King, whom we believe to be the Son of God, the Divine Logos. Those who rule well in the divine nation — that is, the Church, rule in accordance with the divine commands. They never allow themselves to be led astray by worldly policy.

So it is not for the purpose of escaping public duties that Christians decline to hold public offices. Rather, it is so they may reserve themselves for a more divine and necessary service in the Church of God — for the salvation of men.

The Unstoppable Spread
Of Christianity

"Go ye therefore, and teach all nations, baptizing them
in the name of the Father, and of the Son,
and of the Holy Ghost." Matt. 28:19

Our numbers are continually increased by the addition
of converts from the worshippers of [pagan] gods. Yet, even
in persecution itself, our numbers are never lessened. For
truth prevails by its own power. **Lactantius**

Notice the contrast between human philosophy and
Christ's gospel. Although philosophy remained primarily
in Greece, the words of our Teacher did not remain in
Judea alone. Rather, his words were scattered over the
whole world, over every nation, village, and town. It
brought individuals and entire households over to the
truth. In fact, it won over quite a few of the philosophers
themselves.

It is worthy of note that if some ruler prohibits the
teaching of Greek philosophy, such teaching immediately
vanishes. In contrast, our teachings were prohibited from
the very beginning by kings, tyrants, rulers, governors,
and all sorts of men who warred against us. In fact, they
tried to exterminate us. Yet, our teachings only flourish
all the more. For the teaching of Christ does not die out as
does human teaching. **Clement**

There is no nation so uncivilized, no region so remote,
that neither Christ's Passion nor the height of his majesty
would remain unknown. For that reason, in his suffering,

he stretched forth his hands and measured out the world.
He thereby showed that a great multitude, collected
together out of all languages and tribes, from the rising of
the sun even to its setting, was about to come under his
wings. (Rev. 7:9) **Lactantius**

All who once shared in your ignorance and hatred of
the Christian religion shed their hatred as soon as they
came to know what it is. What's more, they actually
become what they had formerly hated. And now they hate
what they had once been.

Day after day you groan over the increasing number
of Christians. Your constant cry is that the state is beset
by us. You complain that Christians are in your fields,
your camps, and your islands. You grieve over it as though
it were a calamity that each sex, every age, and every rank
is passing over from you to us.

Still, you love to be ignorant of what other men rejoice
to have discovered. You would rather not know the truth,
for you cherish your hatred. It's as if you are aware that
once you know the truth about us, your hatred will
certainly come to an end. **Tertullian**

There is not one single race of men, whether barbarians, Greeks, or whatever they may be called — whether
nomads, wanderers, or herdsmen living in tents — among
whom prayers and thanksgivings are not offered through
the name of the crucified Jesus. **Justin Martyr**

Almost the entire world is better acquainted with what
Christians preach than with the favorite opinions of
philosophers. For who does not know of the statement that

Jesus was born of a virgin? And that he was crucified. And that many have faith in his resurrection? And that a general coming judgment has been announced, in which the wicked are to be punished according to their deserts, and the righteous are to be duly rewarded? **Origen**

Christians do not hesitate, as far as it lies in them, to take necessary measures to spread their doctrine throughout the whole world. Some of them have accordingly made it their business to travel not only to cities, but even to villages and country houses in order to make converts to God.

And no one could maintain that they did this for the sake of gain, for sometimes they would not even accept necessary sustenance. Or if they had a necessity of this sort, they were content with the mere supplying of their needs — even though many were willing to share their abundance with them. **Origen**

25

An Invitation

"Let the thirsty come, let anyone who desires it, take the water of Life without price." Rev. 22:17 Moffatt

The following is an excerpt from a letter Cyprian wrote to a Roman proconsul who was savagely persecuting Christians.

While there is still time, make provision for your safety and your life. We please God more by not avenging our wrongs. For we are forbidden to hate. Therefore, we entreat you, while you still have the power — while you are still alive — to make satisfaction to God. We urge you to emerge from the abyss of dark superstition into the bright light of true religion.

We do not envy your comforts; nor do we conceal the divine benefits. We repay your hatred with kindness. In return for the tortures and punishments that you inflict on us, we point you to the way of salvation. So believe and live! You who persecute us, come and rejoice with us for eternity. Once you have departed from here, there is no longer any time for repentance. There is no possibility of making satisfaction. It is *here* that life is either lost or saved. It is here that eternal safety is provided for by the worship of God and the fruits of faith.

No one should hold back because of the amount of his sins or because of advanced age. So long as you are still in this world, no repentance is too late. The approach to God's mercy is open. The access is easy to those who seek and apprehend the truth. Entreat God for the forgiveness of your sins — even though you may be at the end of your life, even though the sunset of your life is at hand.

Implore God — who is the one true God — in confession and faith, acknowledging him. Pardon is granted to the man who confesses. The divine goodness gives saving mercy to the believer, and opens a passage to immortality even in death itself. Christ bestows this grace. He bestows this gift of his mercy by overcoming death in the victory of the cross, by redeeming the believer with the price of his blood, by reconciling man to God the Father, and by reviving our mortal nature with a heavenly rebirth.

We are made by him into the children of God. We shall live forever with him. With him we shall always rejoice, restored by his own blood. We Christians shall be glorious together with Christ, blessed by God the Father. We shall be always rejoicing with perpetual pleasure in the sight of God, ever giving thanks to God. For no one can be anything except forever happy and grateful, who once having been subject to death, has been made secure in the possession of immortality. **Cyprian**

The average Christian knows more about the history of his country than he does about the history of Christianity.

We're out to change that!

We believe the Bible is the only inspired Word of God. However, there are over 300 denominations today that claim the Bible as their only source of authority — yet they all teach widely differing things. In light of this, we believe the best way to accurately understand the Bible today is to go back to the writings of those men who heard the apostles preach or who were taught by the disciples of the apostles.

When a person searches back to early Christianity, he soon discovers that we live today in a topsy-turvy spiritual world where orthodoxy is called heresy and heresy is called orthodoxy. A world where the commandments of Jesus are often ignored but the commandments of men are treated as though they were sacred. But please don't take our word for it! Read the witness of the early Christians firsthand for yourself.